LESSONS FROM THE EDGE

LESSONS FROM THE EDGE

ISBN (paperback): 978-1-968919-34-4
ISBN (ebook): 978-1-968919-33-7

ARMINLEAR

Armin Lear Press, Inc.
215 W Riverside Drive, #4362
Estes Park, CO 80517

The stories that appear in the 10 inserts in this book were taken from *Heart of a Stuntman,* Kevin Ball's first book.

LESSONS FROM THE EDGE

where the world taught me to belong

KEVIN BALL

CONTENTS

INTRODUCTION

Stuntman! I read the word aloud. I'm proud of the label—proud of my hard work, bumps, and bruises. I even appreciate the macho image associated with being a professional Hollywood stuntman. It has been a long, challenging journey to reach my current status: respected among my peers and regularly employed.

But through divine intervention and the workings of the universe, I began to earn another title, one that surpasses even the mighty stuntman: humanitarian. Being a humanitarian has taught me more about embracing vulnerability and openly loving others than I ever could have imagined. Combining these two professions creates a formula for balance and patience, unyielding strength of heart, and, as I have experienced, a greater understanding of the world and what the universe offers each of us. These two careers reflect each other in both adventure and danger, but only one fuels my drive to move forward each day and help those at risk. They need us so their voices can reach our ears and hearts.

It was mid-May 2014 when I received a call from Jim to work on *Terminator Genisys*, the next action saga in the *Terminator* franchise. Arnold Schwarzenegger was back in this time-traveling prequel, and I was ecstatic about the opportunity to contribute to such this highly anticipated 2015 summer blockbuster. The interesting thing is that this time I knew exactly why I was here; I could trace the events that led to my trip to Louisiana, the location for this film. My journey began with a humanitarian mission to aid the refugees of the 2013 Typhoon Haiyan disaster in the Philippines, rather than my usual hustle on Hollywood movie sets.

It was a sweltering night. We were about twenty minutes outside the heart of downtown New Orleans, and the post-apocalyptic military wardrobe I wore only added to the discomfort of the evening's rising humidity and temperature. The long-sleeve olive-green army jacket and cargo trousers had been distressed by applications of stiffening fabric paints, which constantly irritated any skin they contacted, scraping and chafing my unshaven neck nightly. Bulky nylon waist packs and ill-fitting custom plastic body armor compounded the discomfort and hindered my ability to move, run, and fall accurately. Many of those actions occurred each night, and all three are very important in the stunt world. Then there were the cheap leather Chinese combat boots issued by wardrobe, so stiff that they creased wherever my foot flexed, creating sharp edges angling inward. I empathize with the Chinese military and assume that everyone in the country must be flat-footed due to the total lack of arch support. If not for the pricey orthotic gel inserts I bought from a Bourbon Street pharmacy, I'm almost certain I would be slightly crippled from the ankles down right now. And, of course, we were shooting all night scenes. This caused my mind to slip in and out of mild states of delusion—something you don't want when you're running from special effects explosions large enough to engulf a high school football field. Humans aren't designed to sleep during the day; three nights in, we were all getting a bit loopy.

The sequence we were filming, set thirty years in the future, portrayed a group of rebels, led by a future John Connor, attacking a Skynet prison encampment amidst the rubble of a destroyed LAX airport.

The impressive set was constructed in a massive gravel quarry adjacent to the dikes of the Mississippi River, which flowed only about fifty yards to our east. The set was divided into two areas. The first was the Skynet prison camp, guarded by the iconic silver humanoid endoskeletons we've all come to identify with the name *Terminator*; the second was the bombed-out ruins of LAX airport. The ruins included enormous piles of broken concrete strategically arranged by the set design team to create paths large enough for our rusty, custom-built attack vehicles to navigate through and over. The rubble was scattered with fragments of airport and airplane debris, reminiscent of an airline crash site. There were luggage carts, sheet-metal covers from jet engines, and entire sections of plane wings large enough to climb on and run across. Goodyear tires nearly as tall as I am were still attached to sections of shattered landing gear. Even full lengths of dismantled 747 fuselages, complete with cockpits and rows of passenger seats, were laid out for us to use as giant props. It was a disaster-zone playground for stunt performers.

The prison camp set was more elaborate and featured dozens of 40-foot silver monolithic structures designed to function as holding cells for the humans captured by the terminators. Each freestanding structure had a rectangular base nearly the size of a shipping container, with three slightly smaller sections stacked on top, tapering as they ascended, to achieve the total height. This tapered shape provided stability to the structures and enhanced the megalithic imagery. Between every two structures were fictional red laser fields that kept the human prisoners corralled. The result was a stunning creation; one that would soon be consumed by fire and deadly explosion.

On this particularly uncomfortable, mosquito-infested evening, we found ourselves in the midst of some unnerving stunt sequences. The nights prior had built up to this enormous scene—the final attack on the Skynet prison camp—and the special effects department spared no expense when it came to the detonations and fireballs that engulfed the set this night.

A one-hundred-yard perimeter was established as a safety zone for all personnel not directly involved in the scenes being filmed. This mostly included everyone except the pyro-technicians triggering the explosions and us, the stunt team. Two other stunt guys, a stuntwoman, and I were stationed at the base of one of the aluminum-colored containment walls and received specific instructions on when and where to advance. Twenty other stunt people were spread out in various locations with their own cues to move out. Together, we would create the impression of a large siege on the compound.

As if this weren't enough, two colossal six-wheel military vehicles, affectionately called Goers, would lead the advance, followed by half a dozen customized rebel vehicles fabricated from bits and pieces of trucks, cars, and whatever else the designers could weld onto them to achieve the post-apocalyptic *Road Warrior* look. To top it off, two helicopters were in action: one military helicopter with rebel soldiers firing at the terminators from above and a second used for filming. This created a recipe for total chaos and potential disaster. The timing for this shot had to be perfect, not only for the safety of the entire stunt team involved but also because of the significant amount of time required to reset everything if the filming did not go perfectly.

Huddled at the base of our monolith, we realized precisely where we stood in the chain of events to come: helicopters, giant military Goers, rebel vehicles, fiery explosions, and, at the bottom, us—the stunt rebel foot soldiers.

Reality slapped us in the face when the safety team began clearing everyone out of the area—except us. Crew members leaving the chaos passed our little stunt quartet hunkered down in position and gave us that look: "*Well, it was nice knowing you.*" Some offered a fist bump; others wished us good luck while patting us on the back, and some just ran to a safe zone. Moments later, it was just the four of us, all slightly on edge. Through the radio in my pocket, we heard the call to commence the scene. The helicopters took flight and jockeyed for position, while the revving engines of the Goers and other vehicles merged into a stereophonic growl on our right and left sides. Fifteen feet behind us, the metal pipes carrying propane—flame bars—erupted, raising the ambient temperature by over a hundred degrees, and sometimes, when the breeze shifted, the flames taunted us from as close as five feet away.

It was getting hot, uncomfortably hot, and loud, with our only exit leading directly into the mock war zone. The earplugs I wore muffled the sounds but distorted everything to a dreamlike state, allowing me to hear my own breathing above all else. The images of human bodies huddled together and frozen in stone from the ancient volcano at Pompeii flashed through my mind, because we four were unintentionally mimicking some of their poses to escape the heat.

"Three, two, one, action!" the director shouted over the radio, and everything came alive.

BOOM! BOOM! Two of the largest explosions went off in the background, illuminating the set as if the sun had suddenly risen to a noon sky, while filling the air around us with the scent of sulfur and burning gasoline. Increasing pressure in the fuel lines caused the fire from the flame bars to double in size, casting our shadows on the wet asphalt before us. Even with the heat rising behind us, we had to wait until two vehicles passed, triggering a propane explosion placed about thirty feet in front of us. That was our signal to go. With a loud crack and a brilliant flash of fire, the propane popper blew, and we made our way into the war zone.

Splitting up to give the illusion of a greater number of rebel troops, we made our way deeper into the frenzied scene.

I matched the pace of one of the vehicles and pretended to use it for cover as I fired round after round from the heavy Russian AK-47, modified to resemble a futuristic plasma rifle, I carried There was so much happening—fire and smoke, explosions showering us with debris, and gunfire erupting from the weapons mounted on the vehicles or fired by the stunt rebels in front of and behind me. Concentration was paramount. It may just be a movie set, but the explosions are real, and one step in the wrong direction can kill you. The drivers were trying to hit their marks without running us over, but they were as caught up in the chaos just as we were.

Even the simple act of running forward and shooting a rifle becomes complicated with so many other stunt people around. The expanding fiery gases from an AK's barrel can blind a person and are strong enough to blow a chunk out of an ear if you get too close. This was as close to war as you could get without engaging in combat. The big difference, aside from the blank rounds in the guns, is that it all stops as quickly as it starts, with the shouting of one simple word: "Cut!"

I stopped, calmly remained where I was, and checked out the situation around me, a skill honed by stuntmen. The mental relief was evident, spreading across the faces of all the stunt players as the applauding crew began to enter the now safe set. I glanced back at the destruction we had created and felt a twisted sense of pride for being fortunate enough to be involved in such an incredible event.

Jim, a childhood friend and the stunt coordinator who had hired me, approached with the same sense of relief evident on his face. I was one of only three stunt guys that Jim had personally requested for this scene. Not because I had anything particularly special to offer, but because the universe had recently brought us back together. Jim and I had always been great friends; we had started in the movie business together. However, he lives in Los Angeles, and I live in Orlando; the entire country separates us, and sometimes it's just difficult to find the time to connect. But we were both enjoying this opportunity, an opportunity that had arisen by chance because of a deadly storm on the other side of the world. As I looked around, my worlds merged a bit; the scene around me eerily reminded me of the destruction from the typhoon I had witnessed about six months earlier. Yet again, the universe was reminding me of just how interconnected we all are on this planet.

On November 8, 2013, Typhoon Haiyan carved a devastating path through the central Philippines, impacting nearly thirteen million people. My phone rang off the hook. Randy, a business partner who runs a disaster relief and logistics NGO, was heading in to conduct preliminary assessments and wanted me to document the humanitarian mission. For some time, my life outside of getting blown up on movie sets has been dedicated to the passion that fuels my soul: working with international humanitarian organizations. What I have to offer, besides a big heart for those in need, is a background in filming and an uncanny ability to get myself in and out of locations around the world that are anything but tourist destinations. This time, it was a disaster brought on by a superstorm that devastated a peaceful culture of people.

Without enough time to fully consider what I was getting into, I responded to Randy with my usual answer regarding humanitarian work: when and where. A couple of weeks later, I found myself thirty thousand feet above the Pacific Ocean, downing beers and trying to induce sleep during the twenty-three-hour flight to Manila.

Life moves quickly if you let it, and mine was once again accelerating rapidly. I would soon meet up with Randy; we would spend the night in Manila and then find safe passage to Cebu, where our local contact would somehow get us to the devastated city of Togo. There, we would join an Israeli medical team at a makeshift relief clinic and assist with medical assessments using a high-tech portable satellite-based system that Randy had brought. It's called a BGAN (Broadband Global Area Network). The laptop-sized unit connects to a satellite and broadcasts a wireless dome over an area large enough for medical teams and relief workers to send vital information to established hospitals worldwide. It is invaluable during disasters because the first thing to go is always the ability to communicate from the ground.

Day one in Cebu, and I somehow found myself gaining access to a closed-door United Nations (UN) meeting at the aid distribution facility on Mactan Air Force Base. The UN and the World Food Program had selected this site to fly shipments of aid into the hardest-hit areas affected by the storm's brutal path. Mactan itself had been transformed into a temporary refugee camp and human relocation center, in addition to serving as a centralized hub to receive and store international aid shipments.

The runway resembled a used car lot filled with multinational C-130 cargo planes, each marked with its corresponding country's name and unique insignia. The day before Randy and I arrived, a nightmare unfolded. The Philippine government, relying on just one laptop with a spreadsheet of flights, had assumed control of the entire humanitarian operation, dismissing the US military representatives who managed the daily logistics of delivering tons of international food donations to the city of Tacloban. Tacloban was one of the hardest-hit locations in the Philippines, but due to the availability of a functional runway and its central location within the island chain, it became the hub for distributing food and supplies to the refugees affected by the typhoon.

The meeting opened my eyes to the political absurdity of international humanitarian relief efforts. It was one enormous pissing contest, with different entities vying for the chance to say, "We gave more!" The starving and dying people in the flooded streets, along with the women and children being assaulted, were the least important items on the agenda. After an hour of listening to the heartless rivalry, I realized that the only thing that matters is one human helping another. Governmental egotism about how much each country has given to the poor, hungry natives is worthless.

I didn't sleep well that night. I sought comfort in half a bottle of Jose Cuervo tequila that I had packed for just such an occasion and woke with renewed hope that we would be able to do more than just watch international relief leaders play Monopoly with human lives. Over breakfast, we decided to pile into the back of a local's mini truck and drive six hours to a town near the tip of Cebu Island. This area had also taken the brunt of the typhoon's strength, but because it didn't have an airport, CNN couldn't get in. The world didn't know of its dire needs.

A six-hour drive through a disaster zone, in the four-foot-long bed of a Mitsubishi mini truck, with another person and a full load of relief supplies, might seem like a dreadful situation to be in. Not to me. I was back in my element! I held on to whatever I could find for support with my left hand while alternating between video and still cameras with my right. I did what I do best: I documented everything. There is no better way to understand another culture and learn about its people than by fully immersing yourself. Death and destruction surrounded us. Villages were leveled. Trees the size of mighty oaks and weighing thousands of pounds were snapped at the trunk like toothpicks, sometimes with each half on opposite sides of the two-lane road and sometimes crushing small indigenous huts. But like a budding spring rising after the harshest winter, the people were already rebuilding their lives. Even with the deforested landscape surrounding them, the smiles and laughter of the Philippine children echoed through the streets as they ran alongside our tiny blue truck, yelling, "Hi Joe!"—a greeting that survived long past the US military occupation of the Philippines. Only days after the storm's destructive force, I felt a sense of tranquility and beauty.

We finally reached the hospital grounds in the town of Togo. A brown military surplus tent served as the clinic, and we immediately set up the gear and prepared to do what we could to help. It was a chaotic scene! Power lines were down, and toppled trees, broken glass, and trash littered the small town. At times, I felt helpless. I would have loved to do more, but Randy continued to tell me that assessments like ours would greatly benefit future humanitarian aid efforts attempting to reach overlooked locations like this one. From what I had seen of the uncoordinated attempts by governmental organizations, it seemed clear that small groups of thoughtful individuals could be much more effective than even the might of greedy nations. Oh, how I wanted to stay in the Philippines a bit longer, but I only had a few days left, and with my return flight home approaching, it was now time for me to take charge and say "Cut" on this scene of my life.

Back in Manila, you would never have guessed that a superstorm had struck the island chain; life continued as usual. On the morning of my flight, I woke up very early, checked out of my simple hotel, and walked through the dark, bustling streets to hail a cab to the airport. The scents of the morning penetrated the hot, damp air, mingling the aromas from food vendors with oils, exhaust, and the stench of open sewers. At five AM, the traffic was already so thick that walking to the airport might have been a better option, but I craved the experience of a cab ride in Manila one last time. With plenty of time to spare, I checked in, passed through customs, and ventured out to find a cup of coffee and a light breakfast. However, karma had one last surprise in store for me.

Due to an oversight while booking our flights, Randy had accidentally scheduled me for a thirty-one-hour layover in Los Angeles. As I was twenty-four hours ahead of the California time zone this meant I would be spending three full days in LAX airport, one of which was Thanksgiving. As I sipped my strong black coffee and helped a young mother with three small boys pick up some breakfast cereal from the terminal floor, I mentally weighed my options. I concluded that I didn't have many choices. I have friends living in Los Angeles, but reaching out to one at five AM, a day ahead and on the other side of the world, was no small task. Jim was the first person who came to mind, but with his busy schedule, I wasn't going to place any large bets. In the terminal, on the boarding ramp, and from my seat, I sent emails and Facebook messages to as many friends as I could think of, right up until the flight attendant asked me to turn off my Blackberry. From that point on, it was up to the universe to decide my fate, and it didn't let me down! Upon landing in Beijing, China, I turned my phone back on and hit the lottery!

Jim was never one for long messages, but this one read: "Home for the holidays, love to see you. A limo will pick you up. What time do you land, buddy?" Divine intervention was opening yet another door for me, and all I had to do was walk through it. So I did.

The flight from Beijing to Los Angeles was undoubtedly the most taxing part of my journey from Manila. By taxing, I mean long and arduous; in coach, the best thing you can do is shut your brain down and become an air-bound vegetable. However, even with my long legs cramping in economy seating, knowing that I had a makeshift home waiting for me at LAX and that I wouldn't be eating Thanksgiving turkey from an airport vendor's kiosk while alone made this thirteen-hour connecting flight much less mentally taxing. Additionally, I would get to see one of my best friends again. I napped well.

Comfortably numb, my brain switched back to the on position as our plane made its final descent into LA. That Thanksgiving held more meaning than I can ever remember; the compounded emotions from what I had just experienced in the Philippines and my unexpected rescue by my best friend truly filled my soul's love tank.

I stayed an extra week to help Jim reorganize one of his stunt equipment trailers, only to find out about the new feature film for which he'd gotten the stunt-rigging contract: a long-awaited summer 2015 release titled *Terminator Genisys*. I happily accepted his invitation to work with him.

SECTION I

THE ADVENTURE CONTINUES

The universe vibrates with an intricate web of interconnection that transcends human understanding. What may seem like a tragic or desolate event can be a doorway to extraordinary realms of possibility, waiting for those bold enough to embark on the journey and unveil the wonders that lie just beyond the horizon.

In 2009, while documenting the inaugural Operation Smile mission in Guwahati, India, I was moved by the words of an American nurse. Although I do not know her name, I can never forget what she said. Before the mission began, she gathered the entire team—doctors, nurses, students, and volunteers—into the courtyard of the third-world hospital and handed each of us a small stone. She then stated, "*Each of these stones represents one of you. No two are alike; each one has its own unique qualities, just as all humans have unique qualities. If we all go to the river and throw our stones into the water, something happens. The stones will sink, but each one starts a ripple on the surface of the water. While our individual stones may never touch, the actions they create do. Each stone, like each person, generates a ripple in life, moving outward and touching all other ripples, touching all other humans. Actions are interconnected; we are all interconnected; the world is interconnected!*"

In some ways, this is a continuation of my last book, *Heart of a Stuntman.* It contains tales of amusing and enlightening adventures, but it also explores the knowledge I gained from years of experiences that compelled me to look deep inside myself. I questioning the things I have lived through and witnessed, wondering if there were answers regarding empathy, humanity, and the human condition that could guide me to seek out others in need. Over the years, recurring situations, questions, and conversations have led me to identify theories that can be integrated into everyday life. I hope to inspire others to venture forth with a thirst for spiritual illumination. The journey will encourage you to step into the unfamiliar in search of that sunset beneath an African sky, a sunrise on a Haitian beach, or wherever it is your heart dares to go. By embracing the unknown and abandoning your fears, you will set yourself free.

Universal Declaration of Human Rights

Whereas recognition of the inherent dignity and the equal and inalienable rights of all members of the human family is the foundation of freedom, justice, and peace in the world,

Whereas disregard and contempt for human rights have resulted in barbarous acts which have outraged the conscience of mankind, and the advent of a world in which human beings shall enjoy the freedom of speech and belief and freedom from fear and want has been proclaimed as the highest aspiration of the common people,

Whereas it is essential if a man is not to be compelled to have recourse, as a last resort, to rebellion against tyranny and oppression, human rights should be protected by the rule of law,

Whereas it is essential to promote the development of friendly relations between nations,

Whereas the people of the United Nations have, in the Charter, reaffirmed their faith in fundamental human rights, in the dignity and worth of the human person, and the equal rights of men and women and have determined to promote social progress and better standards of life in larger freedom,

Whereas Member States have pledged themselves to achieve, in cooperation with the United Nations, the promotion of universal respect for and observance of human rights and fundamental freedoms,

Whereas a common understanding of these rights and freedoms is of the greatest importance for the full realization of this pledge,

Now, therefore,

The General Assembly,

Proclaims this Universal Declaration of Human Rights as a common standard of achievement for all peoples and all nations, to the end that every individual and every organ of society, keeping this Declaration constantly in mind, shall strive by teaching and education to promote respect for these rights and freedoms and by progressive measures, national and international, to secure their universal and effective recognition and observance, both among the peoples of Member States themselves and among the peoples of territories under their jurisdiction.

A short rant

The text above serves as the *preamble* to the *Universal Declaration of Human Rights*. The United Nations Declaration outlines thirty articles that define human dignity. You should read them. I believe this is merely the tip of the iceberg. I think this or another declaration should encompass education, clean water, basic sanitation, medical aid, and food. *Shouldn't access to water and food also be considered basic human rights?* I still find it hard to comprehend that there are places on this planet where a child can be born, and their greatest killer lurks not in the shadows but in the parasites of unclean water.

Diarrhea kills 2,195 children daily—more than AIDS, malaria, and measles combined. This accounts for 1 in 9 child deaths worldwide. Statistics like these, along with those on poverty, war, sex trafficking, and a multitude of other issues, can easily be found with a simple Google search. Can it be depressing or discouraging to read? Certainly! It can keep you awake at night.

However, when you educate yourself about human issues, you become more human, more empathetic, and more aware of the basic needs that are easily within your reach at this very moment.

Access to clean water is a fundamental human right! Yet millions of people in developing countries face the daunting challenge of obtaining safe and reliable water sources. The lack of clean water threatens the health and well-being of individuals and communities, hindering social and economic development. Clean water scarcity is a significant problem in many developing nations, where communities struggle to obtain water free from pollutants, bacteria, and other contaminants. The consequences of this crisis are dire, as unsafe water leads to waterborne diseases such as cholera, dysentery, and typhoid fever, causing illness, suffering, and even death.

Several factors contribute to the water crisis in developing countries. The main challenges include inadequate infrastructure, limited resources, and population growth. Deficient water storage and distribution systems, along with a lack of sanitation facilities, perpetuate the cycle of water-borne illnesses. Furthermore, pollution from industrial activities and poor waste management worsens the situation by contaminating available water sources. The absence of clean water has severe health implications, especially for vulnerable populations such as children and older adults.

Waterborne diseases weaken the immune system, making individuals more vulnerable to infections. This raises morbidity and mortality rates, affecting the overall well-being and productivity of communities. Moreover, the responsibility for water collection often rests on women and children, who must spend hours each day gathering water instead of pursuing education or engaging in income-generating activities.

The water crisis also presents significant economic and educational challenges. Access to clean water is essential for communities to maintain proper hygiene, which impacts productivity and economic growth. Frequent illnesses and hospitalizations deplete financial resources that could otherwise be allocated to education, infrastructure, and other vital areas.

Moreover, the burden of water collection frequently prevents children, especially girls, from attending school, perpetuating the cycle of poverty and restricting opportunities for future generations.

Addressing the clean water crisis requires a multifaceted approach. It begins with investing in infrastructure development, including the construction of wells, pipelines, and water treatment plants. Governments, NGOs, and international organizations can collaborate to enhance water management systems, raise awareness of hygiene practices, and promote sustainable water use.

Applying innovative technologies and purification methods can also make a significant difference in ensuring access to clean water in isolated areas. Education plays a vital role in addressing the water crisis. Communities must also have access to information about the importance of clean water, proper sanitation practices, and methods to maintain water quality. Educational campaigns, workshops, and awareness programs can foster behavior change and promote sustainable water use. Moreover, advocating for policies and funding that prioritize clean water initiatives in developing countries is essential for establishing long-term change.

NGOs such as Water.org and Lifewater.org are two organizations focused on water that are genuinely making a difference in global clean water advocacy and development, though there are many more. Access to clean water is a fundamental human right that should be available to all, regardless of geographic location or socioeconomic status.

Each time I return from a mission in a country with potentially unsafe water, I find myself refusing to take water into my mouth while in the shower. This action (simply putting my face into the stream of water flowing from the shower head), or lack of action, heightens my awareness of how challenging conditions are in many places worldwide.

Just pause and look around; there's likely clean water nearby, food within reach, and most likely, nobody is shooting at you. Only when you acknowledge how incredible your life is, according to human rights, can you take a deep breath, truly open your eyes and heart, and reach out to help another.

I don't say this to guilt anyone into joining the Peace Corps, selling all their possessions, or giving everything to charity. However, knowledge genuinely is power. Even in the worst conditions, children still laugh and play, while families love and worship with hearts full of hope. Yes, desperation exists, but so do hope, faith, passion, and love. I've witnessed it firsthand. I have, and will continue to, preach this from my soapbox: *Humanity is simply one hand reaching out to help another in need. Nothing more! Nothing less!*

In the Cary Grant movie *That Touch of Mink*, Grant's character, a millionaire philanthropist, addresses the United Nations. I listened to his short speech once and had to rewind several times to write it down. I don't know who originally wrote it, but it resonated deeply with me.

> *"The wealth of a nation is in the well-being of its people, both spiritually and materialistically. It's not a question of lowering our standards but of helping others to raise theirs. If all people everywhere can be content, and their living standards even and compatible with ours, there would be no envy in the world and, therefore, less provocation of war. When you encourage and help people to develop their own natural recourses, you do more than put bread in their mouths; you, put dignity in their hearts."*

Beyond the introduction

Carefully perched on a homemade wooden box haphazardly strapped to the bed of a tiny blue pickup truck, my head and shoulders towered over the truck's cab as we sped down the mountain road through the cool morning air. Describing our mode of transportation as a truck is a slight overstatement; it was indeed a truck, yet so much of it wasn't at the same time. The Suzuki "Carry" Mini-Truck sported the same three-cylinder, 660 cubic centimeter engine found in their lower-end motorcycles. Its cab was home to two non-adjustable bucket seats that forced your back to remain erect against the truck's oversized rear window. If you were fortunate enough to have shorter-than-average legs, your knees had less than six inches of space before they were firmly pressed against the hard plastic dashboard. The resemblance between the space in the truck's cab and a budget airline coach seat was uncanny. The truck's bed measured four feet wide and a bit less than five feet long. There wasn't much space left after we added the three plastic crates of disaster relief supplies we'd brought into the country, our backpacks, my video camera equipment, Allan, myself, and the wooden storage box we were seated on.

I was working with a nonprofit relief organization called Disaster Logistics Relief (DLR), and we were on the island of Cebu in the Philippines, assisting with relief efforts ten days after Typhoon Haiyan cut a swath of devastation across the belt of the island chain.

Our happy little quartet consisted of me, Randy Roberson, self-proclaimed disaster guru, my business partner at DLR, Allan, a thirty-year-old evangelical Baptist minister, and Skip, our local contact on the island of Cebu. Skip ran a local mission in the mountains of northern Cebu and acted as our liaison with the Philippine military, the government, local NGOs, the US military, and United Nations officials. He was also rather intimidating—scary, to be precise! A military veteran of both the Iraq and Afghanistan conflicts, Skip had survived being blown up more than once. He suffered from a severe case of PTSD, or Post Traumatic Stress Disorder, as well as active shell shock that caused him to jump at the slightest surprise or random loud noises. After working with multiple military branches, Skip ended up at the US Department of Defense and the Central Intelligence Agency, participating in several black ops missions worldwide. He was a trained killer and a top CIA interrogator; it was nearly impossible to read his emotions.

He was also what one would call a large-framed individual, able to shift from a blank, deeply thoughtful stare deep= to a chuckling grimace in the blink of an eye. Usually wearing a tight red T-shirt, tan shorts, and sandals, he resembled a younger version of Santa Claus on a permanent tropical holiday, though minus the long white beard.

Allan's only mission in life seemed to be ministering to anyone who would stand still long enough for him to climb up on his invisible pulpit and quote the Bible. He could pull out biblical passages to correspond to our situation faster than anyone I had ever met and often sounded like a Christian auctioneer. Randy told me this was Allan's first time outside the US, aside from an organized missionary trip to South America. A disaster zone in the Philippines was a new experience for Allan. This became evident daily at breakfast when, after unsuccessfully trying to find something more American to eat, he would excuse himself early, step outside, and try to convert the hotel doormen to the wonders of Christianity. Allan didn't drink alcohol, did not use profane language, believed homosexuality was a sinful addiction that could be corrected, and tried to convert me more than once. But deep down inside, once you got past that and his Amish-looking hat, he was a really good guy.

I had only been home for a little shy of a week after a less-than-fulfilling film job in Puerto Rico when I received the call from Randy that we needed to get over to the disaster zone. As much as I hate to admit it, I longed to be back in a natural disaster situation. In Puerto Rico, I stunt-doubled for the actor John Cusack in a movie titled *Reclaimed.* It was about human trafficking, a subject that is near and dear to my heart. It had been a very slow year in the film world, so I was just happy to have a job, at first. Then it turned into a situation with no communication, no budget, and no certainty about how safe things would be. You don't want to end up in a hospital in PR after being crushed in a poorly fabricated roll cage, placed in the barely running vehicle that you are supposed to drive. I wanted out, and Randy's call gave me that option.

Randy and I had met a couple of years prior when I was trying to find a literary agent for my first book, and we were both almost drawn into the same scam. A very unscrupulous individual tugged at our empathetic heartstrings, using a handful of legitimate humanitarians to raise money for his ill-gotten gains. We removed ourselves from the situation but stayed in touch; it seemed the universe had something in mind for us. Eventually, we formed our own non-profit, 501 (c), and with help from a few other kindred spirits, Disaster Logistics Relief (DLR) was born.

Now, we were rocketing down a mountain road in Cebu in a clown car, searching for an Israeli medical relief camp near the town of Togo.

Randy had been at every major global disaster site in the past twenty years; his specialty was logistics and the emerging field of telemedicine. That's what DLR did: logistics, communications, and telemedicine. A simple explanation is that we would go in immediately after a disaster struck, conduct assessments, and relay the needs of the affected people to international and government aid groups. Additionally, we would set up medical camps where we used wireless Internet devices and satellite equipment to stream live medical examinations from the disaster zone to doctors anywhere in the world, or as our mission statement reads,

> *"Our mission is to save lives and reduce suffering for the victims of disasters and for those in humanitarian crisis both in the US and around the world by deploying the best in advanced mobile medical technologies and emergency management."*

Sounds pretty impressive, right?

A Compelling Personal Truth

A day after Randy, Allen, and I landed on the island of Cebu to assess the damage caused by Typhoon Haiyan, we were invited to attend a very closed-door meeting with officials from the United Nations World Food Program. Once again, I found myself blankly staring up at the sky, wondering, "Now, just how did I get here?"

Mactan Air Base served as the staging location for the joint international response to humanitarian aid arriving in the Philippines. From Mactan aid was flown to Tacloban, one of the hardest-hit areas in the island chain. This site was selected because Tacloban had an operational airfield and provided easy access for CNN and other news outlets to generate a significant media surge. As long as the primary global media channels are present in a disaster zone, donations continue to flow; when the media loses interest and withdraws, two-thirds of the international humanitarian aid dries up. It's a sad but undeniable fact. Mactan Air Base is where I began to learn a *personal truth* that would haunt me for many years. However, it was also one of the most crucial lessons I would learn about global disasters and the challenges surrounding the logistics of delivering aid to those in need.

By dropping a few names, presenting some outdated International Red Cross (IRC) credentials, and taking advantage of the chaotic environment, we easily breached the air base's security. Randy reached out to an old friend who was the military contact for the multi-international aid distribution efforts. This guy decided what went where and on whose plane.

Days earlier, before we left the US, we were informed that we would have access to any international aid flight arriving in Tacloban and, even more importantly, to returning flights. Exiting a frenzied disaster zone is sometimes more difficult than getting into one; with the surge of refugees struggling for a way out, aid workers often find themselves stuck on the ground much longer than they wish to be there. To our surprise, we arrived just one day after the Philippine government took over the entire operation and started to push the US and our military personnel out.

Randy's friend and our best hope for organized transportation was one of the first to go, and his replacement was in way over his head. I still find it hard to believe, but the entire Philippine command taking over the multinational relief effort consisted of two Filipino military officers, two hand-held two-way radios, and one laptop computer showing a spreadsheet of flight information. The laptop was connected to a television that sat next to the doors leading out to the tarmac of the airfield where the C-130 cargo planes were staged for loading. We had unknowingly walked smack dab into a massive international clusterfuck.

Randy decided to contact Skip and inform him of our situation. Skip was our ground contact whom Randy had only met a couple of weeks prior through an email chain, but he was extremely credentialed and highly recommended to us in case we found ourselves in a jam. This certainly seemed like a definite jam that could slam the brakes on our entire deployment. Skip suggested that we return to our hotel in Cebu City for the night. He told us that he would be in touch first thing in the morning, after he made a few calls.

Skip lived up to his reputation. Bright and early the next day, he arrived at our hotel in his tiny blue truck and said that he had everything covered. Allen and I climbed into the mini-truck bed, while Randy squeezed into the cab, and we set off back to Mactan Air Base for a second attempt at finding some answers, this time with Skip leading the way.

With a new, handwritten sign that read "disaster relief vehicle" taped to the truck's front window and a very fast-talking Skip, we breezed past the Philippine military guard post and onto the secure air base. Skip navigated the roads as though he knew exactly where he was heading, and within a few miles, we were pulling up in front of the forward operating and logistics center.

We parked alongside a white United Nations van and Skip instructed to hang out while he went to find someone. About fifteen minutes later, he returned with two US military soldiers: one from the Army and one from the Air Force. We were then briefed on the situation. The information we had received the previous day was accurate; the US had been relieved of its command over the joint force of international military aid flights leaving from Mactan Air Base. This information ended of our hopes of catching a flight to Tacloban or any other location on a US military aircraft. The two US soldiers took Skip and Randy inside the command center, while Allen and I were instructed to wait by the truck. I leaned back and closed my eyes for a nap, as Allen seized this moment to rehearse his biblical quotations. A short time later, Randy emerged from the building and headed to the truck.

"Grab your gear, Kevin; a few photo opportunities might arise," Randy yelled as he navigated through the sea of international soldiers separating us. Upon reaching the truck, he told us that good old Skip had come through and pulled some strings to secure a private meeting with the Filipino Army General, who had been in charge of the entire aid distribution operation. This was a huge privilege for a private sector NGO, and Randy was eager to take full advantage of it.

I snatched my backpack from the truck bed and followed Randy into the headquarters, where I found Skip and the General waiting for us. After making introductions, we were led to a small private area offering a great view of the international fleet of military cargo planes loading aid supplies and off-loading refugees from regions devastated by the typhoon. While Randy and the General spoke, I took an opportunity to snap some photos of the ongoing relief work on the tarmac, the activities in the room, current maps with regular updates on where the aid was being distributed, and, of course, some discreet shots of Randy and the General in deep conversation.

The informal conversation lasted about twenty minutes, which was all the time the General had to spare. Cordial handshakes and a grateful thank you ended the conversation; Randy approached me with a pleased smile and informed me that the General had personally invited us to sit in on a private closed-door meeting the following day, a meeting that would truly open my eyes to the world of international disaster relief.

The following day, without Skip's assistance, it took Randy and me a bit of persuasion to talk our way past the same security guards who had barely acknowledged us the day before; Skip certainly has some pull with the local military. Eventually, the three of us—Randy, Allen, and I—were again granted entrance to the airfield, but our cab wasn't. So, we jumped into the back of a military transportation jeep and proceeded to the base to join in on the scheduled meeting. Upon entering the staging office, we were instantly noticed by one of the US military officers whom Skip had introduced us to the previous day. With limited greetings, he hurried our trio past the heavily armed Philippine soldiers guarding the doors and into the conference room.

All eyes were on us as we entered the room, mainly because we were the only three not dressed in military uniforms or displaying United Nations credentials. Randy sat at the large meeting table and was quickly noticed by one of the UN representatives. Had it not been for the recognition and gratitude from the new Filipino General in charge, we would probably have been escorted out. Allen and I chose seats against the far wall of the room and pretended to be invisible; it's surprising how well that often works. As the meeting ramped up to speed, it became clear that a power struggle was developing because the United States no longer commanded the aid operation. Try as he might, the soft-spoken general could not maintain control of the international group.

Let me clarify what was happening and why this represented a profound *personal truth* for me.

Each country's military officers only wanted to fly relief aid from their own country to the disaster site. Perhaps they were all acting under direct orders; I don't know. I could only see what was happening right in front of me.

Germany wouldn't fly France's cargo; Indonesia wouldn't transport China's cargo; India wouldn't carry Brazil's cargo, and so on. Some C-130 cargo planes were taking off half-loaded, while others refused to take off until their planes were fully loaded with relief supplies from their own countries. This situation not only created bottlenecks on the runways but also wasted valuable tarmac space, delaying much-needed aid from reaching victims in critical need. People were dying by the thousands, and the world's governments were locked in a pissing contest to get their country's name at the head of the top doners list. It was a giant publicity stunt. I couldn't believe what I was witnessing, but it was about to get worse. One of the United Nations World Food Program (WFP) representatives, a younger gentleman, obviously not the one in charge, posed a question to the table. "What should we do with the private sector donations?" he asked.

Private sector donations refer to relief aid not supplied directly by a country's government. This may include local Red Cross groups, Rotary Clubs, church organizations, schools, clubs, or any group of private citizens working together to send supplies to help the victims of natural disasters or international refugees.

I will never forget what I heard next. In response to the younger WFP representative's question, the senior representative in charge stated, *"Private sector donations are a low priority; in fact, they are of no priority. Do not load that stuff onto any of our planes. We work in tonnage only. Just leave it on the tarmac; someone will eventually take it."*

Randy, having heard this statement before, during previous missions, glanced my way to see if the comment resonated. It did, and my jaw dropped; even if I could have spoken, I was at a loss for words, which is rare for me. The pilots in the room appeared to disagree with this order, and individual conversations began to fill the meeting room.

In an attempt to get the meeting back on track, a very irritated pilot from Australia loudly announced that he and his co-pilot would personally fly any private aid. Upon hearing this, the WFP lead bellowed, "Fine, it's all yours; I wash my hands of it!" By this point, Allen and I were starting to lose our invisibility cloak, and we were attracting some looks from UN team members. The camera in my hand and the blank, "you must be out of your mind" expression on my face gave us away as outsiders who shouldn't be hearing this conversation. I got Randy's attention, snapped a few last photos, and headed toward the door with Allen close on my heels.

In my wildest dreams, I could never have imagined what I heard in that meeting. But the truth of what happened is now embedded in my mind. I could have read about the meeting, listened to an audio recording, watched a video, or even received a firsthand account from someone present, but none of those experiences would have been the same. Because I experienced it, it has become a *personal truth*!

Insert 1—Cambodia Here We Come/Deadly Steps

After a few days of practice filming and exploring the stunning coastline roads to Big Sur, the day to embark on my first international humanitarian trip finally came. Everyone met at Mia Hamnet's house for a family and friends send off. Mia is the founder of Freedom Fields USA (FFUSA), an organization that had essentially grown from a women's book club. More than a dozen of the women would be part of our party, along with my dear friend and fellow stuntman John Evanko, who had agreed to be part of this life-changing journey

Eventually, the chauffeured vans that would take us all to San Francisco International airport arrived. Wasting no time, we loaded up our gear and we were off. San Francisco is not too far north of Carmel, so we arrived at the international branch of the airport after only a few hours. Our flock unloaded the vans and ventured inside to start the journey of a lifetime. Almost immediately we had our first back out. We had barely passed through the terminal doors when one of the women—who had never been away from her family and kids before, let alone ventured anywhere near where we were going—got cold feet. She just couldn't go through with it and called her husband to pick her up. She simply wasn't ready.

This made me realize just how many people in the US never venture outside their comfort zones. During a dinner on one of our later trips, John said a few words that will stay lodged in my memory forever. We were going around the table answering the question, "What's the one thing you would tell others about your experiences from this trip?"

When his turn came John said, "I wish everyone in the United States would get a passport and just leave; go somewhere they never thought that they would go and just experience life." Our journeys have taken us in and out of many developing countries and I can say for a fact that when it comes to the world, we, the people born in the United States, are the minority. Most people on this planet don't live the way we do and no matter how bad you may think you have it, trust me you don't. There are grocery stores with food in them here and all you have to do is work a job, earn money and buy the things you need. The government doesn't change overnight, so you probably won't wake up one morning and discover that half the country is trying to kill you because your tribal leader was overthrown. Children here can walk to school without fearing they will step on an abandoned landmine. You can drink the water right from the faucet. You don't have to scrounge in winter for scraps of cardboard to fill the holes in your shack in some shanty town. Your first childhood memory isn't of the white UN planes that dropped bags of food from the sky. You don't have to remember the fights that broke out when many of the bags broke on impact and children as small as you were had to fight for nourishment. We in the USA live in an environment that much of the world will never see or understand. That's why it's so important to get out and see things - not to dwell on the suffering and poverty in the world, but to look at your own life in an entirely new light.

The flight to Cambodia was the longest that I had ever taken. I believe it was close to twenty hours from San Francisco to Cambodia, with a quick stop in Taiwan to change planes, and most of it was at night because we were flying east, away from the sun.

When we landed at Siem Rep International airport, the plane rolled to a stop and a member of the flight crew opened the door. Even from the back of the cabin I could feel the heat as it entered the plane. It carried a smell that is uniquely Cambodian. Very early each morning people from households and businesses alike sweep the fallen leaves, sticks, and rubbish that have accumulated during the night to the edge of the street and light the small piles on fire. The result is an almost incense-like smell that takes over the air and lingers throughout the day. It may sound like a foul smell, but somehow these random ingredients combine to create a pleasant aroma that is hard to forget. It's a memory triggering odor and, to this day, smelling something remotely close will take me back to the streets of Siem Rep.

A few days into our stay, and after briefings from Nigel Robinson, our HALO Trust guide, we headed out for our first visit to the mine-fields.

The mines in this area had been laid in the ground as recently as 1993. The huge mine belt called the Kapeia 5, meaning "protect 5 province," or K-5, runs for over 450 miles along the border between Cambodia and Thailand. No one knows the exact numbers of mines in the ground but, at one time, it was estimated that there were over a million. The reason the numbers are so high is because the border between the two countries has changed many times. As recently as 1998, the government of Cambodia would not let the landmines be taken out of the ground because they felt that their presence would stop possible invasions from Thailand.

What the mine belt really did was stop transit between the two countries—the transit that brings in vital goods and services to some of the poorest people in the world. As major cities grow larger and, as they expand outward, the poorest are forced to move farther away from the advancing cities and closer to the inexpensive border regions where these minefields are located. Many countries have this problem, but Cambodia is one of the most heavily mined countries in the world. Very little government assistance is available, so humanitarian organizations remove most of the landmines. HALO Trust is one of the largest of these organizations.

No one kept good records of just where the mines were laid during the conflicts. If there were any maps of minefields at all, no one has been able to locate them. Unfortunately, this often means that the location of these minefield stays a mystery until some poor Cambodian, living or working in the area, steps on a mine. NGOs mostly rely on the villagers as a first line of notification.

Animals often venture into the mined locations first. After an animal trail becomes visible, the locals know that this spot is free of mines and that it's safe to follow. Greater use of the trails inevitably creates a wider path, often leading to a surprising wrong step and contact with a buried landmine. Those who venture off the trails to harvest wood or use the land to plant crops take their lives into their own hands. But they do it to survive. Consider that a man from the inner city can make $1.50 (US currency) a day by harvesting rice during the wet season. This is enough money to make a trip through potentially dangerous minefields worth the risk.

The sobering truth is that, on average, it costs about one hundred US dollars to remove one landmine from the ground, but only about five dollars to put one in the ground. The price created an incentive for governments to continue using these weapons; that and the fact that, from a military perspective, they work. So, economics contributed to a problem that not only touches farmers and commerce but also extends to children trying to walk to local schools. Mines block access to clean well water and impede proper medical support to thousands of families that live around minefields. There are even areas in which parents tether their children to their huts, so they do not walk too far out into their own yards, where buried mines may well be present. What type of life is this for a child?

Land cleared of mines is so valuable that local villagers are always hot on the heels of the HALO demining teams as they clear. Sometimes people follow a team right up to the edge of the danger zone. They start moving in and cultivating the land less than one hundred yards behind the live minefield actively being cleared. This quickly leads to the creation of more small villages and even more people trying to find their way safely through a maze of hidden landmines.

SECTION II

SELF-ACTUATORS

Self-Actuators

In this process of letting go, you will lose many things from the past, but you will find yourself.
Deepak Chopra

The last two words in the previous section of this book are *personal truth*. Personal truth is one of the seven self-actuators I discuss in this book. You may wonder, what are self-actuators?

They are practices that anyone can apply in everyday life to help calm the mind and reconnect with their presence in the larger collective of the universe. These practices are discussed throughout this book; they are drawn from the personal life experiences that the universe has graciously gifted to me.

Self—*An individual's awareness of their own existence or identity; the ego:*

Actuator—*The mechanism that a control system uses to act upon an environment.*

So, in this context, a self-actuator is an environmental mechanism that can directly influence one's consciousness, identity, or ego when acted upon or utilized. The seven self-actualizers, I cover in this book—*Universal Doors*, *Personal Truths*, *Looking at Life Like a Child*, *Apparent*

Dualities/Balance, *Open-Heart Love*, *Shopping Cart Religion*, and *Universal Karma*—are those that stand out to me. However, individuals can discover an infinite number through their own experiences.

You can integrate all of the actualizers you discover into everyday experiences to aid your journey and growth, helping you overcome emotional and spiritual roadblocks. While not every self-actuator will suit each situation, if you consciously practice them all, you will discover the right one each time—the one to guide you along the path of universal balance.

Stunts mirroring life

In the world of professional stunts, we are often called to reenact or create battle sequences. On the Warner Brothers film *Jonah Hex*, we had to blow up a train, an ironclad boat, and nearly every other set in which we appeared. This was a fictional Civil War-era film and bodies frequently flew through the air. In the stunt world, to achieve a realistic appearance when recreating a battle sequence, we use mechanical devices to launch us forward instantly, as well as others that pull us backward. To propel ourselves violently forward, we utilize an air ram, a device that resembles a giant mousetrap.

The air ram lies flat on the ground until the stunt person steps on the trigger plate, causing the ram to kick up instantly at approximately a forty-five-degree angle, propelling the individual into the air in a forward motion. To achieve the opposite effect of violently pulling a stunt person away from an explosion, we use a device called a ratchet.

A ratchet is a long pneumatic piston device, similar to the one that allows your screen door to close, but these ratchets are about one hundred times larger and capable of snapping your spine in two if not used with the utmost caution. I have ridden both often and always need to control my adrenaline levels because after they fire off, you're in for one hell of a ride. Within a fraction of a second, you're trying to figure out which way is up while searching for the ground so you can land on something other than your head. Each of these mechanical devices connects to a firing control box that contains a mechanical actuator, a mechanism that opens instantly, allowing pressurized air or nitrogen to flow into the ram or ratchet, enabling it to perform its physical action. This works much like *self-actuators* that help us quickly open our minds, enabling us to make more balanced decisions and choices in everyday life. These choices can heal emotional pathways and allow humans to follow the loving flow of the universe.

The Universal Door

Do not fear to step into the unknown
For where there is risk, there is also reward.

My father once told me that you couldn't add a single day to the life you were given. Only God knows that number, but you can surely do things to shorten your days. While I believe this is a very true statement, I now know through personal experience that you can speed up your life. Alternatively, you can slow it down due to fear and an unwillingness to let the universe, or God, lead you where it wants. The movie *Yes Man*, starring Jim Carrey, is an entertaining example of this theory. What if we said "yes: to things more often? How would our lives flow? Whom would you meet? Where would you end up? What adventures would you have?

Tell the universe how you want your life to go, and it will laugh. We all grow up with an idea of what we want to be. This thought may change many times during the aging process, but most children, teens, and college students have some idea of a career or path in life. But how many of us actually get there? With luck and hard work, some do achieve their goals. They plan, go to school, and eventually find their dream jobs. However, most who reach greatness often fall into it. Doors open for us every day as we walk this earth. Some opportunities are as simple as saying "yes" to a new type of food or taking an untraveled road that leads to a new restaurant or store. Others are much larger, such as accepting a new job in a different town or country. Joining the military, accepting a marriage proposal—these experiences make life flow faster. They offer us new challenges and force us to let go of the control we think we have over our lives.

Just think about how often you have encountered an old friend or made a random acquaintance; such interactions lead to unique experiences. Your friend might say, "Hey, a group of us are going surfing, and I just happen to have an extra surfboard. You should come along!" A door has just opened. You can decline the offer or step through the open door to a new experience. Either choice is fine; you can't make a wrong decision what you choose serves your needs at that moment. However, one leads to the unknown and a faster-paced life, while the other is safe and keeps us moving more slowly.

Let's say you accept the invitation; what could happen? You might discover a new passion that leads you to travel the world in search of that perfect wave. Perhaps one of the people in the group is a beautiful, free-spirited woman with whom you feel a special connection, paving the way for a date, a relationship, or even a future family. What if someone you meet that day introduces you to a new career opportunity? The possibilities are as limitless as the stars in the night sky. How often have you considered something a fantastic coincidence or wondered, what if I hadn't gone there or done that? Where would I be now? The meaning of life that many people seek is straightforward. Life is a gift of experiences and a constant progression forward. If you allow life to guide you and walk through the doors the universe opens, your life will accelerate, making your head spin. Yet, it will be fulfilling, filled with true adventures. However, it's not as easy as it sounds. Humans crave security, safety, and routine. Fear holds us back from walking through open doors; we fear change and the thought of our lives moving too fast. We have only one opportunity on earth, one life, and many cling to every second, missing out on the wonders that life has to offer.

My first trip to Cambodia was as terrifying as it was enlightening. It was when I began to see doors opening, and, cautiously, I chose to step through them.

Until then, all I wanted was to be a professional stuntman, and I fought tooth and nail for every job I could find. However, fearing change, I clung to my day job at the studios in Orlando and would only venture so far in search of movie work. I envied, and still envy, some of my stunt friends who threw caution to the wind, packed everything up, and simply went out searching for opportunities. Some went to Los Angeles, others to New York, and through persistence and hard work, many of them became highly successful, achieving heights they never thought possible. But I was not ready to make that journey; fear held me back. So, taking the leap and buying a ticket to Cambodia seemed almost insane, but I did it.

I conquered my fear and decided to let the universe control my life. It was a life-changing decision. Honestly, I had no idea what I was doing, but a calming force was at play, almost guiding me through each door that appeared and opened, beckoning me to see what lay on the other side. I planned to make a documentary on humanitarian landmine removal, and when I first stepped into a live minefield, I couldn't believe I was there. Time seemed to speed up, and new experiences surrounded me, yet I still thought it was my decisions guiding me.

It wasn't that at all; my choices had brought me there, but life was pushing me where it wanted me to be. I just never stopped to question it or attempt to slow things down. The epiphany hit me on one of my last days in Cambodia while touring the temples at Angkor Wat. I had what I thought was a chance meeting with Cindy McCain, wife of Senator John McCain. Little did I know that this was no chance meeting; it was life placing me in the precise moment to see if I was ready to step through another door into even more unknown. So, I stepped through, and what awaited continues to amaze me when I think about it.

- A few months later, Cindy McCain called me, and I found myself in Vietnam with the international group Operation Smile.
- Operation Smile then offered me the opportunity to work with them in Kenya during the 25th-anniversary mission, *The World Journey of Smiles.*
- Cindy McCain then took me to Kosovo and Scotland to document the international humanitarian landmine removal organization known as The HALO Trust.
- Through my connection with the group on our first trip to Cambodia, I was invited to travel with a dental NGO to Lima, Peru, where I had the opportunity to visit the Incan ruins of Machu Picchu.
- I then traveled with Cindy McCain through Southeast Asia during the 2008 US presidential campaign in which her husband, John McCain, was a candidate.

- While with the dental group again, I recorded their mission to the jungles of Guatemala and had the opportunity to visit the Mayan city of Tikal.
- I was a personal guest of John and Cindy McCain on election night in Arizona, with access to their family's private suite.
- I was sent to Dubai and India on the same trip to document the World Food Program and an inaugural Operation Smile mission for Cindy's new foundation.
- I traveled to Ecuador with the dental group.
- I have documented over ten missions with Operation Smile in Brazil, Bolivia, Mexico, Paraguay, and more.

During those seven years, I circled the globe, experienced the world's wonders, and was touched by the kindness of humanitarians and the humble families who received help. I laughed, cried, encountered a few sketchy situations, and was amazed beyond my wildest dreams. But the truly remarkable part is that I didn't create any of this; life did. I just refused to be caught up in the vice of fear and never once tried to slow down the pace. My example may be extreme, but it's a genuine illustration of what can happen when you cast aside your fears and bravely walk through the open doors that the universe presents.

In *The Laws of Spirit,* Dan Millman writes, "*When discipline and patience join forces, they become a persistence that endures past the peaks and valleys to carry the intention to completion. Enthusiasm sets the pace, but persistence reaches the goal. Process, patience, and persistence are all keys that unlock the doorways to any destination.*"

Reflecting deeply on this comment and my experiences, I arrived at another question. Do the doors of the universe open without our effort? Is our effort the key to these doors? Does our *patience* unlock them, allowing the universe to reveal its secrets? I believe so. As Lao Tzu said, *"A journey of a thousand miles begins with one step."*

That's the effort: taking that one step and showing the universe that you are ready to be led and that you're not afraid to truly live the life you were blessed with. The journey lies in patience, or faith, as many call it. Not the faith that you will receive everything you want, but the faith that if you let go and bravely move forward, your life will be provided to you.

Insert 2—Angkor Watt and Our New Friend Cindy McCain

On our second to last day in Cambodia John and I decided to venture out to see and film the famous Angkor Watt temple in Siem Rep. Our plan was to get the sun rising behind Angkor Watt. This was supposed to be an amazing sight, and we wanted it for our video archives. After paying our fee to enter the temple grounds we walked over the stone bridge, past the manmade lakes, and through the smaller temple gate entrance to a football field sized courtyard. Somewhere in the darkness, on the other side of the courtyard, sat the Angkor Watt temple complex.

We sat in the dark, waiting for the sun to come up behind the temple complex so we could get mind-blowing shots to add to our soon-to-be award-winning documentary. Slowly it happened: the sky lightened enough for us to lay our eyes on the outline of the massive temple complex for the first time. It was a spiritual vision, and it was much farther away than I thought it was. Also, what I thought was a large courtyard appeared to be something else entirely. Whatever it was, the ground seemed to be moving. The more the sun outlined the temple, the more the ground swayed. Then it began to pulse with small, moving lights flashing in random patterns. What the hell was this? The silence died and we could make out sounds—human sounds, voices, all speaking Japanese! It seems that we had chosen to visit Cambodia during the annual Japanese tourist photography pilgrimage. Half the population of Japan now stood between the temple of Angkor Watt and us.

This is a problem I've found at historic sites and temples around the world. Wherever there is an interesting spot for tourists to visit, there is a place for commerce. Hotels and markets spring up everywhere, competing for the visiting travelers' dollars. Ancient places of worship that are still used by local families are overrun by tourists and their cameras. Money speaks loudly! There is very little concern for the people worshipping at the site or trying to connect with their own history. Worse, tourism can sometimes bring in billions of dollars in revenue to the townships and countries that house these mysterious icons, forcing the poor local families who lived in the area to move elsewhere. Wealthy tourists spending thousands of dollars to stay in a five-star hotel with a view of an ancient temple don't want to see a homeless family cooking dinner over an open fire next door to the million-dollar resort pool. Of course, the locals are often removed using less than friendly persuasion techniques.

Things got better as the day moved on. The temple was incredible and the morning rush for sunrise shots died down to a point that we could film uninterrupted. When we'd had our fill of filming Angkor Watt, we casually meandered back to the temple entrance to search for our tuk-tuk driver.

The timing could not have been more perfect because out in front of the temple, waiting for their car to be brought around, were Cindy McCain and her assistant Wendy. We had met them briefly at one of our first HALO briefings, and this morning they too had gone on a last-minute tour of the temples before they headed to the airport. This was no coincidence if you ask me: karma had John and me in its grips. We chatted with Cindy and Wendy about the trip and about how amazing the temples were. Then, their car pulled up and we said our goodbyes.

Before she got in the car, Wendy pulled me aside and said that Cindy was really impressed with the tenacity and dedication that John and I had shown during our filming and that there might be some stuff coming up in the future where our services might be needed. This was great!

Wendy and I exchanged information, and we waved at their car as it drove away. Then we went back to touring the temples, proud that someone was impressed by our work ethic and that we had made friends with a Senator's wife. The possibility of a future connection seemed appealing but not yet firm enough to consider. I still had a few things to learn about karma and coincidences.

Looking back now, I can see that the one truth in my life at that time is that I continued to step through the doors karma opened for me. Only slowly did I realize that there is no such thing in our universe as a coincidence. Whether or not you believe it, and you might be tired of people saying this, everything happens for a reason - even if that reason doesn't affect you personally at a particular moment in time. Everything I experienced on this journey, from coming up with the idea to create the documentary, to traveling to Carmel and then to Cambodia happened so that John and I would be in that exact spot at the temple complex, at that exact moment, to run into Cindy McCain and Wendy again.

Personal Truths

Give a man a fish, and you feed him for a day.
Teach a man to fish and you will feed him for a lifetime.

While it might seem like a cliché and we while we have all likely heard some variation of it our lives, this statement serves as an example of a *personal truth.* Let's begin by understanding the word true and why it differs significantly from the word truth.

As we grow, we begin to perceive the boundaries of what has been established as accurate. Throw a rock into the air, and it will fall back to the ground. This is gravity, and we all know it to be true; it's a proven scientific fact. All humans breathe air to survive; this is true. As I write this, I am wearing blue denim jeans. Two plus two will always equal four. Something that is *true* is factual; it can be proven to be true. A *truth*, on the other hand, must be lived; it is a personal experience, something from which you walk away with first-hand knowledge that you did not possess before the event. It is the knowledge that now resides within you, and that no one can ever take it away. It creates new memories and can change your perceptions of life.

Let's consider a straightforward example. If you are an adult of driving age, you have changed, or will have to change, a flat tire. Those who have changed a tire now own that *personal truth*. They have gained hands-on experience in removing a flat tire and replacing it with an inflated tire on their vehicle. If faced with a similar situation, they could recall this information, replicate the action, or guide someone else through the process. They have retained that *personal truth*; no one can ever take it away from them. You can read a detailed book on how to change a tire and gain knowledge. You can watch a video tutorial or have a friend explain the process step by step, and you will understand how to perform the action and likely change the tire successfully. However, only when you have experienced the process with your body, mind, and spirit will the *personal truth* of changing a tire be embedded in your essence. This theory holds true for every experience a human being encounters in life.

"Never judge a man before you have walked a mile in his shoes."

This is another statement that is often quoted but almost never understood. The mile in question contains many *personal truths*—things you will only know if you experience the same mile. How many times have you heard a friend say that something doesn't look like it tastes good? This comment makes me laugh because of its naivety and simple distortion of two of the five senses: sight and taste.

Until you have tasted something, you don't truly own the taste as your *personal truth*. Good, bad, spicy, or bland; it doesn't matter. You limit your life experience by choosing not to taste it. All actions in life come with certain rules. I'm not saying you should try things that are known to cause bodily harm to yourself or others, but I am suggesting that you step outside your comfort zone. Unless you get a passport and travel to experience another culture, you will never have that truth within yourself. *Personal truths* will remain out of reach unless you take a chance on a new job, move to a different location, or even drive down an unfamiliar road on your way to work.

We all get only one chance at life; I implore you to experience all it has to offer while pursuing your own *personal truths*, especially regarding humanity. When we, as humans, give—meaning truly give from the heart—a cornucopia of feel-good chemicals is released into our brains. These chemicals, which I will go into more detail about in a later chapter, are a divine gift from the creator, signaling to us that we are doing right. I can describe how incredible this chemical release feels, and I can even tell you that medical professionals agree that the chemistry of giving can do marvelous things for both your brain and physical well-being. Still, until you venture forth and experience this firsthand, you will not fully embrace this *personal truth* for yourself. Let me share from my direct experiences that this is a truth that can change your life forever.

I had come a long way from my early adventures documenting for Cindy McCain, working in landmine fields, and filming with Operation Smile. While my title with DLR was Humanitarian Media and Communication Specialist, I was fully involved in every step of the missions. Once again, I was an open book, full of blank pages, ready to be filled with new knowledge. By allowing life to flow and walking through the doors the universe opened for me, I found myself in a situation I could not have imagined I would be in, much less striven to attain.

In my first fifty years on this earth, I have had more adventures than most people could fit into a dozen lifetimes. I have traveled the globe with international dignitaries, dined with top military leaders, and discussed humanitarian issues with US senators. I have journeyed around the world, experiencing cultures and witnessing extreme wealth alongside extreme poverty on the same mission. I have attended an audience with nuns in the barrios of Lima and four-star generals in the opulence of Thailand's five-star resorts. I have been under the watchful eyes of the US Secret Service and navigated minefields with a security team from the British SAS (Special Air Service Regiment). To say that I have amassed a wealth of worldly knowledge is an understatement. Everything I have learned, comes from personal experience and forms my own *personal truths.*

Insert 3—Filming My First Facial Surgery

For some reason John and I always seem to land in foreign countries at night, leaving us with no idea what the landscape looks like. All we see are dark streets lit by an occasional roadside light. That was our initial experience of Ho Chi Minh City. We had been in Louisiana filming stuns for a movie, when, through her assistant, Wendy, Cindy McCain invited us to film an Operation Smile Mission in Vietnam.

We jumped at the chance and after a brief, but intense, period of preparation joined the operation's staff for the nine-day mission, We filmed during the heart-wrenching process in which families were interviewed to determine which children could receive life-transforming surgery during this mission, and the light began to break on the realities of these missions. There were always many more candidates than slots available.

It grew more intense as the Operation Smile staff transformed the operating theater of a small hospital still dependent on American medical equipment dating back to the war into a facility able to handle the complex procedures to follow.

Then came the moment we entered the OR, and the sounds of suction and scraping, and the beep of heart monitors started to echo through my headphones. The smell of sterile tools cleaned by peroxide, betadine solution and alcohol began to mix with the odor of flesh being cauterized. There was also the metallic, gamey smell of blood. Watching a child's face being opened to expose the bone that needs to be carved in order to create a stronger structure is not the easiest thing to view, but, after a short time, I noticed that the video camera acted as a shield between me and the operation. It was going on right in front of me, but I had to focus on the shot quality, the audio levels, and framing out certain things in the monitor—all while not getting in anyone's way.

Cindy and I, in on our scrubs and our lime green sterile sandals, made our way through the hallways of squeaky swinging doors and spent hours filming in the operating rooms. Sometimes there were up to three patients being operated on in one small room at the same time. I remember filming one amazing moment in which a small Vietnamese boy, about ten years old, was walked into the operating room, right through the tables where surgeries were currently going on. He could see the other children lying there, with tubes coming out of them and in a half-dead state induced by the anesthesia. He could hear the same sounds and smell the same smells as we could, but he bravely walked right through the room over to the empty table and, with the help of a friendly nurse, he undressed and lay down for his procedure without as much as a whimper or a tear. As he inhaled the gas coming from the mask placed on him, covering his nose and mouth, the volunteers around him all started to sing *Twinkle, Twinkle Little Star* until he fell asleep. Even though Op-Smile doesn't like to show children being put under anesthesia, this was one of those moments that truly shows the love and compassion these volunteer doctors and nurses bring to these missions.

The filming continued as we moved out of the operating area and made our way down to post-op. Because of scheduling, the children come out of surgery in waves, heading right into the arms of the pediatric nurses that stay with them as they wake from the anesthesia induced sleep. Let me tell you, they all don't wake up peacefully. Kicking, screaming, and trying to pull everything off, or out, of their little bodies is what the nurses are usually greeted with. All while they are trying to check vitals, monitor IVs, stop bleeding, and comfort the children. On more than one occasion we were either given an expressive look, or told outright, "Put the camera down and help me hold this child!" Of course, we always did.

Looking at Life Like a Child

If we all could see the world through the eyes of a child
We would see the magic in everything.
Chee Vai Tang

> *Truly I say to you, unless you turn and become like a child, you will never enter the kingdom of heaven. Whoever humbles himself like a child is the greatest in the kingdom of heaven.*
> Matthew 18:3

What does it mean to become like a child? I am far from being a biblical scholar; quite the opposite, as I believe the Bible and most ancient texts are prophetic interpretations by man. This perspective helps me analyze these verses, as my mind is not caught up in the overall stories of the ancient texts in their entirety, but rather in the hidden and often misinterpreted quotes like this one.

So, what does it mean? And why have many historical and spiritual figures conveyed like-minded thoughts?

> *Grown men can learn from very little children, for the hearts of little children are pure. Therefore, the Great Spirit may show to them many things which older people miss.*
> Black Elk

> *Childhood is measured by sounds and smells and sights before the dark hour of reason grows.*
> John Betjeman

> *Children are natural Zen masters; their world is brand new in each and every moment.*
> John Bradshaw

> *When we learn to see life through the eyes of a child, that is when we become truly wise.*
> Mother Theresa

In the movie *Transformers*, Optimus Prime, leader of the Autobots, speaks of the *all-spark*, a primal energy that brings life to inanimate objects. Not life to the body, but life to the soul.

According to the Mayo Clinic, a baby's heart starts beating just four weeks after conception. This means that the *all-spark*, or in non-*Transformer* terms, the *life force*, has entered the fetus at about twenty-two days. Where does this spark of energy come from? Well, many would assert it's God, but I believe it's the universe. Lao Tzu would refer to it as *The Way*, and it's as ancient as time itself. Some call it Zen, others Chi or Prana, or even simply energy. If you're a fan of Star Wars, it's *The Force.*

> *For my ally is the Force and a powerful ally it is. Life creates it, makes it grow. Its energy surrounds us and binds us. Luminous beings are we, not this crude matter. You must feel the Force around you; here, between you, me, the tree, the rock, everywhere, yes. Even between the land and the ship."*
> Yoda

Regardless of its origin, we must all agree to disagree, for no one truly knows. However, what we cannot deny, as both a scientific and spiritual fact, is that life emerges from a source beyond the realm of human understanding.

If you study for a college final the night before the exam and review your notes the morning of the exam, you will have a closer connection to the correct answers. However, over time, these answers fade from your mind; they become obscured by other focus points. Ten years after graduating, not only do you not retain the answers to all the questions, but most of us can't even remember the names of the professors who issued the exams.

I theorize that the same phenomenon occurs with babies as they grow. Infants represent the closest connection to the origin of the life spark. A six-month-old child is merely twenty-four weeks away from the touch of life. This is an incredible thought! A child possesses a fresh, uncluttered mind. There is no ego, resentment, greed, or malicious thoughts—only love. Love, and amazement at everything they encounter, true awe. There is a perfect balance in their life because babies are always living in the moment, walking through the new doors that open for them, and discovering their own *personal truths.*

As I sit here at a picnic table under a pavilion in one of my favorite parks in Orlando, writing this very book, a giggling toddler—a beautiful little girl of Asian descent—has just run up behind me, filled with enthusiasm over a few multi-colored chalk letters left on the concrete floor, likely artistically drawn by another child who was here earlier. This small child, however, giggled in amazement as her father explained that the oversized pink, green, and white letters formed the word *love.* She was living in the moment. Nothing else mattered in her world. All her focus, attention, and energy, along with all her knowledge, was centered on those four colored chalk letters on the concrete, under a picnic pavilion, in a small park near Orlando, Florida, in the United States, in North America, on planet Earth, somewhere floating in space.

I tell you, that's some damn good focus! Even if you have a clear mind and do many meditation practices, it's tough, if not almost impossible, for us to attain something even close to that kind of focus. We did, however, have it at one time in our lives. We had it in a period before we were forced into a life of timetables and schedules, of meetings and heartbreaks. We had that focused attention on always living in the moment when we were all young children —like this little girl.

Still giggling and stumbling, her tiny pink sneakers, adorned with a white Nike swoosh, swiftly took her to her next moment. It was a sign-post near the parking lot. She touched it, and for a second, it became her everything; her mind drifted into another beautiful, euphoric moment of focus.

Believe me when I say I'm not telling any adult to try to live their life as this little girl is right now, but don't forget that you were once there, too. The next time you find yourself around a couple of infants or young children, quietly observe them. Notice their amazement with every new sight, sound, and touch. Look into their eyes and realize they are our closest link to that original mysterious touch of life force.

Children of the world

My travels have taken me around the globe more than once. Every country, city, and village has its unique way of navigating the ebbs and flows of life. The languages, customs, habits, and conditions may differ, but the children are alike. Their skin color and facial features may not appear the same, but their mannerisms are identical. Even in the harshest living conditions, children laugh and play; they laugh through war and play through famine. Young children forgive quickly and restore balance without holding grudges or seeking reparations and apologies from the future.

On a nutritional level, research shows that infants and even young children know when to stop eating. Their bodies recognize when they have reached the correct caloric intake, prompting them to stop eating—a lesson many adults need to relearn. Countless experts on proper breathing techniques have studied infants and found that they are born with the ability to breathe correctly. Babies breathe through their noses, not their mouths, and if you observe one breathing while asleep, you will notice the rhythmic rise and fall of their bellies as they inhale and exhale. We are born with an understanding of proper breathing, but for some reason, we lose this knowledge as we grow and mature. Isn't it funny how we lose our innate wisdom regarding the proper treatment of our life force as we fill our minds with what we believe is valuable information about human development?

There are many stories about dying people moving toward a white light; they are told so frequently that it's becoming almost a joke. There may not actually be a white light, but in reported near-death experiences, there is always a sense of security, peace, and safety. If a newborn infant could communicate with us immediately after being removed from their comfortable private fortresses of solitude, would they share the same message? Would they speak of the life force?

Let's talk about awe

Awe has always existed. Since the beginning of time, humans have been awe-inspired by sunrises and sunsets. People climb to the top of mountain peaks with the sole purpose of gazing upon vast landscapes. Awe has been the sensation associated with inspiration and is responsible for allowing masters to create their most wonderful works of art. The awe that went into the creation of these sculptures and paintings continues to bless onlookers with their own feelings of awe. It's almost as if awe can be passed on through paint, stone, and wood.

Awe is one of the most profound and mysterious emotions we can experience. It's that rush of wonder, reverence, or even smallness we feel in the presence of something vast, beautiful, or beyond our understanding. Awe pulls us out of our routine thinking. It happens when we encounter something that defies our expectations—like a starlit sky, a breathtaking piece of music, a moment of profound human connection, or a life-altering realization.

When you're in awe, you often feel small—not in a bad way, but in a connected way. Your personal worries, ego, and judgments fade, making you feel part of something bigger—nature, the universe, the divine, or humanity as a whole. Awe slows down time and can shift your perspective. It opens you up mentally, emotionally, and spiritually. Many people describe it as a moment of clarity or even grace.

True awe can bring you to tears or render you speechless. It has a unique ability to reset your priorities, enhance gratitude, and ignite creativity or compassion. You don't have to subscribe to any religious beliefs to experience awe. Science, art, nature, acts of kindness, birth, death—all of these can spark it. Awe reminds us that we don't need to comprehend everything to be deeply moved.

Where does awe come from?

The sense of awe is a complex emotional and cognitive experience that does not originate from a single area in the brain; rather, it involves a network of regions working in concert. Here's what science currently understands:

The Default Mode Network (DMN) is linked to self-reflection, daydreaming, and the sense of self. During moments of awe, activity in the DMN tends to decrease, which helps explain why awe can make you feel smaller, less self-focused, and more connected to something greater.

The prefrontal cortex plays a role in meaning-making, perspective-taking, and the regulation of complex emotions. During moments of awe, it aids in integrating the experience and assigning significance, transforming the moment into something profound.

The Temporoparietal Junction (TPJ) is associated with empathy and directing attention beyond oneself. During moments of awe, the TPJ enables a more outward-focused perspective, reducing ego-centered thoughts, which is a defining characteristic of awe.

The amygdala processes intense emotions such as fear and wonder. During experiences of awe, it activates in response to the intensity or vastness of a moment that inspires awe—especially if it's surprising or overwhelming. The striatum and dopaminergic pathways represent the reward and pleasure zones. These areas may light up when awe is a positive experience—such as witnessing something beautiful or having a spiritual moment—releasing dopamine, the "feel-good" chemical.

So, awe isn't just one emotion: it's a full-body, full-mind shift. It engages emotion, perception, and self-awareness all at once. Awe doesn't just feel amazing in the moment; it actually leaves a trail of effects on your behavior, mind, and body. It can make people more prosocial—kinder, more generous, and more likely to help others. It shifts focus from me to we, encouraging cooperation, empathy, and compassion.

People who experience awe tend to report a more balanced view of themselves—one less ego-driven and more grounded. This can lead to deeper, more meaningful relationships and increased humility. Awe activates a desire to explore, learn, and expand our mental models. It has been shown to boost critical thinking, creativity, curiosity, and openness to new ideas.

It doesn't just affect emotions; it also benefits the physical body. Studies show that awe can actually lower levels of pro-inflammatory cytokines (like IL-6), which are linked to various chronic illnesses, and it may also help reduce physical stress on the body.

It reduces cortisol (the stress hormone). Like meditation or time spent in nature, awe can evoke a parasympathetic nervous system response—slower heart rates, deeper breathing, and a sense of calm. Regular experiences of awe have been associated with lower anxiety and depression, as well as an increased sense of life satisfaction. It fosters mindfulness, gratitude, and even a sense of purpose. A study involving older adults found that taking regular "awe walks"—slow, mindful strolls with the intention of noticing beauty or wonder—results in greater joy, reduced anxiety, and enhanced social connections. Over time, this could lead to improved cognitive and emotional health. Awe acts like a natural reset button for your brain, heart, and nervous system. It reconnects you with what matters, and by doing so, it can shift how you live.

My reason for including awe in the section about looking at *life through a child's eyes* was deliberate; it was carefully considered because when we observe children, we discover awe.

Young children live in a near-constant state of awe, and this is not just cute—it's deeply rooted in how they experience the world. Everything is new; children encounter most things for the very first time—a thunderstorm, a butterfly, a falling leaf, the feeling of sand. Their brains aren't jaded or overexposed. They exist in a world in which novelty is a significant trigger for awe. For kids, the entire world is novel, and they haven't built mental shortcuts… yet.

Adults use schemas—mental shortcuts—to quickly categorize and explain what they see. In contrast, kids have fewer schemas, allowing their minds to remain more open and receptive. Rather than thinking, "That's just a tree," they think, "What is that, and why does it move in the wind like that?"

Young children haven't yet developed a strong, fixed sense of self. They tend to live in the moment, which is where awe resides. There's no ongoing internal commentary, no concern about what's next or what others think, and they question everything.

"Why is the sky blue?" "Where does the moon go?" That natural curiosity prepares them for awe-inspiring experiences because they're unafraid to wonder aloud or admit they don't understand something. Adults often suppress that.

Kids aren't guarded; they feel emotions fully—whether joy, sadness, or wonder—without shame or filter. This emotional openness allows them to be swept away by experiences, as the world hasn't been "explained away" for them yet. Adults lose their sense of awe because they believe they understand how the world works, but awe thrives in mystery and vastness. Kids haven't had that mystery dulled yet—they still believe in magic, wonder, and possibility.

Want to reconnect with that childlike awe?

It often starts by noticing differently; by slowing down, releasing the need to always know, and allowing yourself to feel surprised once more. It's not about being childish; it's about fully engaging with the moment. Reclaiming that childlike sense of awe is akin to awakening your inner wonder. Here are some simple, powerful ways to reconnect with it.

Take awe walks—even short ones. Walk slowly and let your eyes wander. Look up at the sky, the shapes of leaves, the cracks in the sidewalk. Look like you've never seen these things before. Imagine you're seeing the world for the very first time.

Ask questions without needing answers. Kids ask why over and over. "Why do trees grow toward the sky?" "Where does the wind begin?" Let the mystery be beautiful. Watch something in nature… really watch it. A bird building a nest, rain sliding down a window, the stars. Get quiet. Let what you see absorb you. Imagine being a tiny part of that rhythm instead of just an observer.

Listen to music with your eyes closed. Select something that stirs your emotions—instrumental, orchestral, or even ambient. Allow the music to just flow through your body. Children feel music before they fully comprehend it.

Spend time around kids or animals; observe how they explore and play. Allow yourself to join in without self-consciousness. Their wonder is contagious.

Create something without a goal. Paint, scribble, sing, dance, or write—even if it's not good. The point is to play, not to seek perfection. Let your imagination take the lead, just like when you were young.

Visit a place that feels vast or unfamiliar, like a mountaintop, the ocean, an art museum, a concert hall, or a forest. Seek out spaces that make you feel small in a positive way, where you sense you're part of something greater.

Practice cultivating a beginner's mind. Approach something familiar as if it's new—like eating a strawberry, lighting a candle, or washing your hands. Pay attention to the scent, texture, sound, and temperature. Awe often hides in the ordinary.

Let silence in even for a few minutes. No phone, no agenda, no noise. Let your senses awaken. Allow your thoughts to settle. Awe often emerges in stillness.

Tapping into awe doesn't require effort; it requires openness. The more you soften into wonder, the more it manifests.

Therefore, awe is not a rare treasure hidden away in mountaintops or miracles; it is the subtle magic woven into the everyday, waiting for us to remember how to see. It resides in the silence between heartbeats, in the curl of a child's question, and in the slow drift of a cloud across the sky. Awe doesn't ask for understanding—it seeks presence.

To live in awe means to say yes to life, not just as it is but as it could be—mysterious, wild, and infinitely alive. The child within us never left; it has been waiting for us to look up.

Awe is the antidote to saviorism

Saviorism flourishes where awe is missing. Without awe, humanitarian efforts quietly elevate the helper while reducing those being helped. Awe does the opposite; it humbles the ego and amplifies dignity. Standing in Rwanda, I realized that empowerment begins not with what we bring but with what we acknowledge. Awe breaks the illusion that we are the central solution and reveals a deeper truth: real change only occurs when we respect the strength that already exists. Awe is the emotional stance that empowers by removing the illusion of superiority and replacing it with respectful partnership.

Saviorism arises from scale distortion. It occurs when one person's sense of agency becomes larger than the people before them. The helper takes center stage; the person helped becomes a background. Awe corrects this imbalance; it reminds us that we did not arrive first, that we are not the most crucial force in the story, and that life, dignity, and resilience existed long before our involvement. In awe, the self diminishes but meaning grows.

What saviorism feels like vs. what awe feels like.

Saviorism shouts, "Look what I am doing for them." Awe says, *"Look what already exists here."* Saviorism positions the helper above the situation. Awe places the helper within it. That shift changes everything.

The neurological reason this works is that saviorism often runs on dopamine (reward, validation), identity reinforcement, and control. Awe activates the vagus nerve (regulation instead of dominance), oxytocin (bonding instead of hierarchy), and decreases default-mode activity (less ego narration). In awe, the brain literally becomes less self-referential. You are neurologically less capable of centering yourself. That's why awe produces reverence instead of rescue fantasies. Awe redefines the role of the humanitarian.

Without awe, humanitarian work whispers, "They are broken. I am capable." With awe, the posture becomes, *"They are resilient. I am invited."* That invitation matters.

Empowerment only works when it honors existing strength, not imagined deficiency. Saviorism rarely announces itself loudly. It doesn't usually come with arrogance or bad intent. More often, it slips in quietly, disguised as kindness. It appears when help becomes part of identity, when doing good revolves around the helper instead of the person being helped. Saviorism isn't born from cruelty; it's born from a skewed perspective—when one person's power grows bigger than the dignity of those they want to help. Awe corrects that imbalance. Think of saviorism as a situation in which a person donates or volunteers and then posts about it on social media for likes and admiration. Awe leads to an internal feeling of accomplishment without the need to boast about it for self-gratification.

Awe occurs when the world feels larger than our personal story. It breaks the internal voice that says, "I am the answer here." Instead, it brings a gentler, more truthful realization: *"I am a witness, a participant, a guest."*

At sunrise and sunset in Rwanda, I noticed that awe arrived uninvited. The land didn't perform; it simply existed—layered with history, resilience, and quiet persistence. Life moved forward without asking for permission or validation. Saviorism didn't feel offensive; it felt absurd. The idea that I had come to fix something collapsed under the weight of what was already whole, already functioning, already dignified. That collapse matters. Saviorism depends on hierarchy, subtly positioning one group as capable and another as lacking. Awe dismantles it by shrinking the ego and expanding meaning. When awe is present, the helper no longer stands above the story; they are placed inside it. This is not a metaphor. Neurologically, awe reduces activity in the brain's default mode network. In plain terms, awe makes us less obsessed with ourselves. It activates the vagus nerve, encouraging calm and connection rather than dominance or control. It increases oxytocin, the hormone tied to bonding and trust. *Awe doesn't prepare the body to conquer; it prepares it to relate.* That shift changes how humanitarian work gets done. The attitude shifts from, "You are broken, and I am here to fix you" to, "*You are resilient, and I am here to learn how to stand beside you.*" The difference is subtle in words but profound in effect. Empowerment cannot flourish in the shadow of superiority—even when it's well-intentioned

In Rwanda, awe reshaped my understanding of strength. This was not a place defined solely by what it had suffered, but by what it had chosen to build afterward: order, vision, and forward motion. Dignity expressed itself not through grand gestures but in everyday life. The people here were not waiting to be saved; they were already shaping their own story. That understanding brought tears—not of guilt but of humility. Tears fueled by awe evoke a different emotion. They aren't fueled by shame or pity but by recognition—the recognition that dignity existed long before my arrival and that my role, or at best my contribution, was only a single thread, not the entire fabric. *This is where empowerment begins.*

Empowerment isn't about transferring power from the capable to the incapable. It's about recognizing and strengthening the power that already exists. Awe helps us see that power clearly. It trains us to notice what is working instead of what is lacking, who is leading instead of who is struggling, what has endured instead of what has been lost. Without awe, humanitarian work often relies on urgency and emotion— particularly guilt. I have seen the emotion of guilt overtake entire groups of volunteers on their first international missions. Guilt can prompt action, but it rarely fosters wisdom. Guilt-based giving seeks relief, often for the giver. Awe-based engagement seeks understanding. It slows us down enough to ask better questions: *What is already thriving here? Who should be leading this effort? How do we support without replacing?*

These questions don't arise from strategy alone. They stem from reverence. When we are in awe of a place or people, we stop seeing ourselves as essential. We become optional—and that is a gift. Systems that depend on outsiders to function are fragile. Systems that appreciate local leadership last. That's why awe leads to better results, not just better intentions. It encourages partnership rather than prescription, collaboration instead of control, and sustainability instead of dependence. Awe teaches us to approach communities with curiosity rather than conclusions.

Rwanda, stripped away the illusion that meaningful change begins with just arriving. It reminded me that genuine contribution starts with listening, with restraint, and with the humility to recognize that we are joining something much older and wiser than our own plans. Saviorism claims, "Look what I am doing for them." Awe, on the other hand, says, *"Look what already exists here"* That difference influences everything that follows.

Awe is not passive. It does not justify inaction or indifference. Instead, it purifies motivation. It bases humanitarian work on respect rather than rescue, on dignity rather than dominance. Awe keeps the focus where it belongs—not on the heroism of the helper, but on the humanity of those being served.

Ultimately, awe is not a feeling we indulge in; it is a stance we take. It is the emotional discipline that makes empowerment possible. Without it, we risk confusing our presence with progress. With it, we learn to contribute without taking over, to support without overpowering, and to work toward a future where our absence doesn't mean collapse but signals success.

In Rwanda, at the edges of sunrise and sunset, I felt my sense of self loosen. Awe does that—it gently displaces the ego and replaces it with belonging. The tears that came weren't just grief or joy, but recognition. Recognition that life is vast, fragile, and dignified all at once. Those tears were my nervous system bowing—not in weakness, but in reverence. They reminded me that empowerment begins when we stop standing above the world and start standing within it.

Tears of awe

Awe is one of the rare emotions that shrinks the ego while expanding meaning. Standing in Rwanda at sunrise or sunset—the land quiet, light spilling across the hills, life moving without asking your permission—my brain wasn't just seeing beauty. It was recalibrating itself.

Neurologically, awe does several remarkable things. It decreases activity in the default mode network—the "me, my story, my worries" loop—and activates the vagus nerve, promoting a state of calm connection. It also boosts oxytocin levels, enhancing feelings of belonging and softening the boundaries between observer and observed. That's why awe often feels both humbling and intimate at the same time.

Why does awe often cause tears?

Awe expands the mind beyond its current limits. Psychologists call this cognitive vastness—when something is too big, too beautiful, or too meaningful to fit neatly inside us. Tears appear when meaning exceeds language; gratitude meets humility; beauty brushes against mortality. In those moments, crying isn't sadness—it's integration. Your nervous system releases emotional tears because words aren't enough, but connection still needs an outlet. Those tears in Rwanda were my body saying, "*This matters more than my defenses.*"

The chemistry behind tears caused by awe

Awe-related tears often include (oxytocin)—fostering bonding with people, places, and life itself, and (endorphins)—creating a quiet euphoria mixed with reverence. They also lower cortisol after being released, turning stress into perspective. That's why awe-tears feel pure rather than heavy. They don't drain you—they clarify you.

Why this matters for humanity and empowerment is that awe does something radical. It reminds us that dignity isn't earned—it's inherent.

When I felt awe in Rwanda, I wasn't just moved by the landscape or wildlife. I was standing in a place layered with resilience after devastation. A place with human stories stitched into the soil, and where life continues with quiet courage. Tears in that context are a recognition of shared humanity—not pity, not distance, but kinship. Empowerment begins right there. You can't empower people you see as abstract. Awe collapses that distance, and tears seal the understanding.

The fundamental chemical composition of human tears

Human tears are more than just salty water—they act as a small biochemical message from your body. Their precise composition varies depending on why you're crying, but here's the basic chemistry.

The basic chemical makeup of human tears is 98-99% water. This acts as the solvent for everything else and keeps the eye surface smooth and protected. Sodium (Na), Chloride (Cl), Potassium (K), and Bicarbonate (HCO3) are the electrolytes that give tears their familiar salty taste. Tears are slightly hypertonic, having a higher osmotic pressure than blood plasma.

Tears also contain proteins and enzymes that protect and heal the eye. *Lysozyme* kills bacteria, *Lactoferrin* binds iron to prevent microbial growth, *Lipocalin* stabilizes the tear film, *Immunoglobulin A* (IgA) provides immune defense, and *Growth Factors* assist in tissue repair.

There are also hormones and signaling molecules that are especially present in emotional tears. *Cortisol* (stress hormone), *ACTH* (Adrenocorticotropic hormone), *prolactin* (responsible for lactation, breast development, and hundreds of other actions needed to maintain homeostasis), and *leucine enkephalin* (natural pain-relief peptide). This is why emotional crying can feel physically calming. There are also *lipids* (oils) that prevent tears from evaporating too quickly and help keep vision clear.

However, not all tears are chemically identical

We have *basal tears* that are always present, mainly composed of water, salts, and protective proteins. *Reflex tears* are triggered by irritants like smoke or onions; they contain more water, fewer proteins, and hormones, and are intended to wash away irritants. *Emotional tears,* on the other hand, contain higher levels of stress hormones and neurotransmitter-related peptides, which are chemically distinct, not just more abundant. The main scientific takeaway is that emotional tears physically help remove stress from the body. They represent a mixture of chemistry with meaning—part immune response, part emotion, and part repair mechanism.

Why humans cry emotional tears, while most animals do not

Crying functions as a social cue rather than an indication of weakness. Emotional tears evolved primarily to benefit the community rather than the individual. Tears play three crucial roles at the same time: they expose vulnerability, foster empathy, and reduce aggression in others. Research indicates that witnesses to tears are more inclined to offer help, less likely to react angrily, and more prone to trust the person crying.

In evolutionary terms, tears convey, "I'm not a threat. I'm hurting. Stay with me." That's how survival depends on connection. Tears trigger empathy in others. When someone sees another person cry, their mirror neurons activate, their anterior insula lights up (emotional sharing), and oxytocin increases (bonding humans). Tears are essentially biological subtitles for pain—they translate inner suffering into something others can instantly understand.

How often have you heard someone say, "Now, don't start crying. If you do, I'll start crying too." Tears aren't contagious physically, but emotionally, they can be. Consider this: the same chemicals in a mother's breast milk that foster bonding between mother and child are also found in our emotional tears. This shows that humans are naturally inclined towards compassion, empathy, and kindness.

Crying helps regulate the nervous system. Emotional crying usually occurs after prolonged stress, not during moments of peak danger. Chemically and neurologically, the parasympathetic nervous system activates, causing the heart rate to slow down afterward, stress hormones to decrease, and endogenous opioids (natural painkillers) to be released. That's why post-cry exhaustion often comes with feelings of calm or clarity. Your body is essentially saying: "We survived. Stand down."

Why animals don't cry emotionally

Animals definitely experience fear, grief, and attachment—but they don't depend on complex social repairs as humans do. Showing vulnerability can be risky in the wild, and their emotional communication is more about behavior than symbolic gestures.

Humans, on the other hand, based survival on long childhoods, interdependence, moral bonds, and shared meaning. Tears became part of our moral language. The deeper meaning is that emotional crying sits at the intersection of dignity—acknowledging pain matters—of humanity—suffering is shared, not isolated—and empowerment—vulnerability creates connection, not weakness. Tears say, *"I am affected by the world, and the world affects me."* That's not fragility—that's moral awareness. Tears are the body's refusal to let suffering go unnoticed. They are chemistry shaped into a plea for connection—proof that being human means we were never meant to carry pain alone.

Insert 4—The Wonder of Tooth Brushing in Guatemala

Our plane touched down in Guatemala City in the early afternoon, and we were met at the airport by a member of the local organization, Asociacion Rescate, the NGO that International Health Emissaries (IHE) paired with on the ground in the Rio Dulce River area, deep in the Guatemala jungle. Asociacion Rescate's mission is to improve the health and education of the Indians who live in the area. Specifically, this mission would focus on a dental clinic both to provide care and education on oral hygiene. Together we set out on our journey to the selected site.

Sunrise and sunset on the Rio Dulce are both metaphysical experiences. One comes with coffee and the other leaves with a margarita, but both the morning and evening sky are masterpieces of celestial art. Our destination was the point where the Rio Dulce began its journey from Lake Izabel to the Caribbean. There a small army of volunteers constructed the clinic.

They decided that the shade beneath a very large tropical tree in the side yard was the perfect place to set up the teeth brushing classes, where Terry, one of the volunteers, taught the children how to avoid the plaque monster with a song and a wiggle dance that the children adored. Laughter is the best medicine after all, and the children never knew that they were learning. By wiggling and dancing, Terry taught them the perfect technique to get their new toothbrushes into just the right spots along their gum lines. I couldn't get enough of watching these adorable Guatemalan children giggling and trying to brush each other's teeth. They would practice on themselves, they would practice on each other, they would practice on the walls, trees, rocks, and anything that would sit still long enough—including yours truly sleeping soundly in a hammock.

Yep, one day I made the mistake of being so exhausted that I took a catnap in the hammock that hung from the porch overlooking the lake. Now normally this would have seemed like the logical place to slumber for a bit, and, were it not for the close proximity of the cute kids practicing their brushing skills, it might have been the perfect spot. But, in my dog-tired state I slept like a rock, and didn't feel the small lime green toothbrush enter my mouth until it was too late. Ask me where that toothbrush had been moments before entering my mouth or what was on it, and I can only answer with a shrug and a blank expression. But there it was, moving back and forth along my pearly whites. It was not so much the sensation that woke me up as much as it was the adorable giggling of the small boy holding the damn thing in my mouth. There were two boys, I believe. One was the mastermind and the other was helping with instructions and encouragement. Both were about six, one was a good half a foot taller than the other and they were both dressed in their jeans and best going-to-town button-up shirts. As my eyes slowly opened and over tiredness let me wrap my brain around the ongoing activity, I could do nothing but stare at them with a look on my face that must have asked, "Is that the same toothbrush that you were using on the dog twenty minutes ago?" To them I was the perfect practice dummy, my face was at their level and I wasn't moving. With the brush still in motion, I turned my head fifteen degrees to face the future dentist and tried to smile. He found this action hilarious because his giggles turned to full, high-pitched laughter and he and his partner in crime ran away, removing the lime green brush from my mouth with all the gentleness of, well, a six-year-old Guatemalan boy. After a couple good spits, I couldn't help but notice that my wonderful friend John Evanko was immensely enjoying the entire event as it unfolded right there in front of him.

Shopping Cart Religion

> *A place for everything; everything in its place.*
> Benjamin Franklin

Shopping cart religion is a term that I coined in my mind one day as I observed a father and son leave a Lowes hardware store pushing a cart loaded with items they had just purchased. I was passing close enough to hear the two speak as they approached their vehicle, opened the back door, and unloaded their purchases onto the seat. What stuck in my mind was what the young boy told his father as he stared at the now empty cart they had haphazardly pushed to the wayside, front wheels popped up on the six-inch curb to keep the cart from rolling back into the parking lot. With the mental capacity of a Buddhist scholar, that young boy told his father that he would like to return the cart to the storefront where they had initially found it. In a very paternal way, the father said that was fine with him but inquired why the boy found it necessary to return the cart and not just leave it perched. *"Because that's where it belongs,"* said the young boy. Upon hearing this, my heart swelled, and I almost wanted to reward the boy not only for his actions but also for being able to see a reality in life.

"Because that's where it belongs." This statement is so simple to understand and so complicated that many of us, especially when we get into our mid-life era, don't comprehend it anymore.

Let's take our shopping cart as an example. Where does it live?—Where does it come from? In the early morning, when most stores that use carts open for daily commerce, all of the store's carts usually start the day inside the store, conveniently located just beyond the automatic opening doors. Or, in some larger box stores, in neat rows nested within each other under the front awning. As the shopping day continues, the carts make it to and from the parking lot in an ebb and flow of movement. Sometimes the accumulation of carts becomes greater in the car lot, causing an attendant or store associate to venture out, even in inclement weather, to retrieve the carts and return them to the storefront, where the process repeats itself many times throughout the day. What if everyone who went shopping and used a shopping cart that day emulated the young boy's actions?

What would happen if we all just put things back? *Because that's where they belongs.*

Since we are here now, let's focus on the shopping carts. First, if each person who used a cart returned it to the store, it would save the time of the young men and women who have to retrieve the carts each day, possibly allowing their time to be put into something much more productive. We would see less vehicle damage due to unguided four-wheel baskets setting off on their own in search of a previously undented vehicle door panel. The surprise of pulling into a parking spot only to find one or more carts taking up just enough room that the length of your car, truck, van, or SUV won't fit as intended would cease to exist, alleviating a heightened negative emotion and sometimes elevated blood pressure. And the entire parking lot would feel less like a gauntlet to navigate and more like a calming environment in which to park your vehicle. I know all this might seem silly, but if you consider what the young boy said, you realize that only positive side effects would result from returning carts to where they belong. Not to mention the impact that this kind of action has on the subconscious mind. Simply doing something because it's the right thing can have benefits many people never knew existed. The mind and body are flooded with feel-good chemicals and activating them doesn't take much.

According to an article on the Cedars-Sinai medical website on "The Science of Kindness," little actions like putting something back where it belongs can positively impact your life:

> *"The warm feeling of well-being that washes over you when you've done something kind isn't just in your head. It's in your brain chemicals, too. Kindness can release hormones that contribute to your mood and overall well-being. The practice is so effective it's being formally incorporated into some types of psychotherapy."*

Under the title "Kindness Chemicals," the researchers report:

> *"Most research on the science behind why kindness makes us feel better has centered around oxytocin. Sometimes called "the love hormone," oxytocin plays a role in forming social bonds and trusting other people. It's the hormone mothers produce when they breastfeed, cementing their bond with their babies. Oxytocin is also released when we're physically*

intimate. It's tied to making us more trusting, generous, and friendlier while lowering our blood pressure. Acts of kindness can also give our love hormone levels a boost, research suggests. Studies have also linked random acts of kindness to releasing dopamine, a chemical messenger in the brain that can give us a feeling of euphoria. This feel-good brain chemical is credited with causing what's known as a "helper's high." In addition to boosting oxytocin and dopamine, being kind can also increase serotonin, a neurotransmitter that helps regulate mood.

"The good news is that a simple act of kindness can reward our bodies and minds with feel-good chemical substances. However, the effect is short-lived. A single act of kindness isn't going to carry you through several days—or even hours.

"The trick you need to know: Acts of kindness must be repeated.

"Biochemically, you can't live on the 3-to-4-minute oxytocin boost that comes from a single act.

"That's why kindness is most beneficial as a practice—something we work into our daily routine, whether in the form of volunteer work, dropping coins into an expired parking meter, bringing a snack to share with your officemates, or holding the elevator for someone. The rewards of acts of kindness are many. They help us feel better, and they help those who receive them. We're building better selves and better communities at the same time."

So unknowingly, this young boy, through the kindness of his simple action, released a cornucopia of healing and feel-good chemicals into his young brain. But that's not the reason that he did it. He wasn't looking for the natural chemicals; he was doing it because it was the right thing to do in his eyes. Why can't we all be this way?

In a world often filled with stress and negativity, the simple act of smiling and practicing kindness can have a profound impact on our physical and mental well-being. Research has shown that these seemingly small gestures can lead to remarkable improvements in our overall health. Let's explore the science behind how smiling and kindness positively affect your health.

The chemical compounds of humanity

The saying "Smile and the world smiles back at you" has a scientific basis. When you smile, it not only lifts your mood but also has a contagious effect on those around you. Mirror neurons in our brains cause us to mimic the expressions we see in others, which means your smile can trigger smiles in others. This positive feedback loop can create an environment of happiness and reduce stress for everyone involved. Smiling has been linked to the reduction of stress hormones, including cortisol. When you smile, your brain releases endorphins and other feel-good neurotransmitters, which can counteract the adverse effects of stress. Lower stress levels contribute to healthier cardiovascular and more robust immune systems.

Kindness and positivity can strengthen your immune system. Acts of kindness trigger the release of oxytocin, often called the "love hormone." Oxytocin has anti-inflammatory effects and can enhance your body's ability to fight off infections. A positive outlook on life is also associated with a more robust immune response. Believe it or not, smiling and practicing kindness can have a pain-relieving effect. Endorphins, released when you smile, act as natural painkillers. Moreover, studies have shown that when patients receive kind and empathetic care from healthcare providers, they often report less pain and recover more quickly.

A positive attitude, often accompanied by smiling and kindness, has been linked to a longer lifespan. People who maintain a positive outlook on life tend to make healthier lifestyle choices, such as eating well and exercising regularly. These habits contribute to better heart health and overall longevity. Kindness is not only beneficial to those receiving it but also to the person performing the kind act. Acts of kindness release dopamine, a neurotransmitter associated with pleasure and reward. This can lead to improved mental health, reduced symptoms of depression, and increased feelings of happiness.

The power of smiling and kindness to positively impact our health cannot be overstated. These simple acts have far-reaching effects on our physical and mental well-being, reducing stress, boosting the immune system, managing pain, promoting heart health, and enhancing our overall quality of life. So, let's make a conscious effort to spread smiles and kindness. Remember, a single smile or act of service can brighten someone's day and, in turn, improve your health and happiness.

Have you ever performed a selfless act? Something really selfless, like an act the person you helped will never be able to repay? Did you give a stranger your coat because the evening was turning cold and they were without warmth? Or did you play Santa for a family without the means to buy Christmas presents for their own children? Or, did you go on a mission trip to some country where the poverty level is extremely high and the needs are many?

Have you ever felt the warm, emotional sort of high that penetrates your body and mind from such an act? It's the inner feeling of peace, connection, and love for others that can be attributed to chemicals produced by our own brains. A person can actually get high from helping; although the high doesn't last for a long time, it's very powerful when experienced.

One of the kindness chemicals that make us feel this way is oxytocin, the love hormone. Oxytocin helps the brain form social bonds with others and has even been linked with allowing humans to trust other humans. Mothers produce oxytocin when breastfeeding, which is transferred to their babies to help strengthen the mother-child bond. Blood pressure, due to the release of both oxytocin and serotonin, lowers when one is engaged in altruistic actions too. Let's also not forget our good friend dopamine, a chemical messenger in the brain that can give us a feeling of euphoria. Add all of these brain chemicals together and you might realize, that human beings are genetically designed to receive one hell of a mood-heightening cocktail during selfless acts of kindness. These feel-good brain chemicals are credited with triggering what's known as a "helper's high."

Where else can these drugs be found and what do they do for the body and brain?

Oxytocin

Oxytocin is sometimes referred to as the "love hormone" or "love drug" for its roles in sexual bonding, parenting, and other social behaviors. It is available by prescription under the brand names Pitocin and Syntocinon, and has been promoted as a wonder drug that can help enhance positive feelings and social skills, while alleviating serious cognitive, psychiatric, and behavioral conditions—including depression and post-traumatic stress disorder. It is also called the "cuddle hormone" as it is also released during social bonding activities, such as hugging, touching, and forming emotional connections. It promotes feelings of trust, empathy, and bonding, playing a significant role in human relationships and social interactions.

Dopamine

Dopamine is a neurotransmitter that helps send signals in the brain, playing a role in the brain's reward system. It helps to reinforce certain behaviors that result in rewards. Dopamine creates feelings of pleasure. Certain drugs, such as cocaine, can cause large amounts of dopamine to flood the system, producing euphoric effects or a high that leaves the user wanting more. Known as the "reward chemical," dopamine is released when we experience pleasure or achieve goals. Acts of kindness can trigger dopamine release, providing a sense of satisfaction and reinforcing the behavior. It is critical for motivation, reward, and reinforcing pleasurable behaviors.

Serotonin

In addition to its link to depression, serotonin may play a role in other brain and mental health disorders, including anxiety disorder, obsessive-compulsive disorder (OCD), post-traumatic stress disorder (PTSD), phobias, and even epilepsy. Serotonin is sometimes known as the "happy chemical," because it appears to play an important role in regulating mood, and low levels of serotonin in the brain have been associated with depression. Examples of prescription forms are Zoloft and its generic form Sertraline, known as Selective Serotonin Reuptake Inhibitors (SSRI) This neurotransmitter contributes to feelings of well-being and happiness. It is released during positive social interactions and activities that enhance mood, such as acts of kindness and generosity. Serotonin helps regulate mood, sleep, and appetite, and is often associated with feelings of contentment and emotional stability.

Endorphins

Often referred to as the body's natural painkillers, endorphins are released in response to stress or discomfort, as well as during physical activities like exercise—which has earned it the rubric "runner's high". Acts of kindness can also stimulate the release of endorphins, contributing to feelings of euphoria and reducing stress.

Endocannabinoids

These are similar to the compounds found in cannabis and are naturally produced by the body. They play a role in mood regulation, pain management, and overall sense of well-being. Positive social interactions and acts of kindness can boost the production of endocannabinoids.

Norepinephrine

This neurotransmitter and hormone is involved in the body's stress response, but also plays a role in attention and responding to positive stimuli. It can enhance mood and alertness when a peron is engaged in positive social activities.

Together, these chemicals create a complex interplay that enhances mood, reduces stress, and promotes social bonding, reinforcing acts of kindness and human connection.

As you can see, these chemicals help aid the body with the critical functions of regulating how well we feel emotionally. These chemicals are even created by drug companies, they're designed to mimic their natural effects on the brain. Humans crave these sensations so much that people often turn to other things; illegal drugs, extreme sports, deviant sexual acts, and even gluttony, to achieve this highly enlightened feeling. Might this then be an act of divine creation? Are we as humans, by design, given unlimited access to these feel-good chemicals so that we will continue to do good, to help our fellow man? The human body only offers natural rewards when we are doing what we are supposed to be doing to keep our internal workings in homeostasis. What better way to keep humanity growing than by a natural shot of feel-good chemicals in our veins.

Insert 5—Kindness Chemicals in Guatemala

From the clinic near Lake Izabel, John and I accompanied a group of IHE volunteers to a remote village with a secret entrance further along the Rio Dulce and deep in the jungle. Asociacion Rescate had a few small and fast transport boats ready for us to use. These were the typical style boats that were operated on the lakes and rivers of the Rio Dulce to take goods and people around. They were open-topped boats with a stand-up helm in the middle and two rows of seats near the front. Large outboard motors pushed the fourteen-foot crafts through the calm waters effortlessly. When you live on a lake or an island, you have a boat instead of a car. That's just a fact.

Passing through the secret entrance, we landed at a dock with a very nicely constructed boardwalk that led to the village's main center. This consisted of a very colorfully painted school and medical center, both constructed of concrete blocks. These were much more modern structures than I had imagined that I would find this far out in the jungle. Mark Bayless, one of IHE's two founders, explained that the buildings had been built with donations from IHE and a number of other NGOs, as was the well and some fencing to contain the animals. This area served as the village hub. Conversation, hugs, and introductions went on for a short time until Mark motioned for us to follow him to the more primitive area where the villagers lived. Off we went, behind the modern village area and into the jungle on foot trails. We reached the huts and this was the village that I was expecting to see in the middle of a tropical jungle.

What I had not expected was the strange merging of the primitive with modern gadgetry.

What I had also not expected was my introduction to Mark's second passion. The language in this area was a mixture of Ketchi and Spanish, but the language that Mark spoke best was laughter and kindness, which is spoken and understood in even the most remote locations on earth. Add his second passion, magic, and this made him easy to find. All you had to do was listen for the sound of children laughing and follow it to Mark and his magic bag of tricks. Like the Pied Piper, Mark would walk along the trails, followed by the village's children. The farther he walked, the larger his following grew.

> *What I have witnessed with humanitarian volunteers everywhere, especially with the IHE group, is that they have truly found the fountain of youth. They just openly give love, and the love they give away propagates and flow back at them tenfold. This compounding effect of a human being giving love in response to greatest need acts like a fountain of youth on the body and the soul. Grow younger by giving to the underprivileged people of the world. I believe this is another part of the meaning of life that people search for.*

We continued our mission in Guatemala, traveling to locations even more remote and even deeper the jungle. The travel involved was arduous and, on occasion, dangerous but most clinic days, especially in the latter part of the mission, were very mellow. Because of the annual IHE trips, some of these children were getting dentistry that rivaled that received by children living in Beverly Hills. The proof was in the teeth. Day after day, child after child needed only a cleaning or a superficial filling. The volunteer group was rightly proud of this success. Sure, they came down to the jungles to remove some teeth and alleviate pain, but they had been doing this for such a long time that the lessons were sinking in. Because of their dedication to humanitarian aid, the native people were now passing down the knowledge and practices they learned to their children and their children's children. Teeth, along with lives were being saved.

> *"A small group of thoughtful people could change the world. Indeed, it's the only thing that ever has."*
> Margaret Mead

Apparent Dualities/Balance

> *To the mind that is still,*
> *The whole universe surrenders.*
> Lao Tzu

Apparent dualities are also known as universal opposites. This is one of the simplest universal laws to comprehend but also one of the most difficult to master. This statement itself is, in fact, an *apparent duality.* The law of *apparent dualities* means that everything in the universe has an inherent opposite quality or state of being dual; essentially, everything has a dual nature. This principle spawned a movement called Dualism; the doctrine that the universe is under the domination of two opposing principles, one of which is good and the other evil.

Balance must also be included in this chapter because balance is the center point between all dualities. It is the center between Yin and Yang, the pivot point on a scale, neutral buoyancy, or the location between positive and negative. Why is this topic so important? Because it's a constant in everyday life and one hundred percent unavoidable. However, if you learn to embrace the law of *apparent dualities* and understand how to find the balance in extremes, your mind will be freer, and your life will flow much more smoothly.

If I were to ask the question, What is the opposite of hot? most adults and even children would answer that the opposite of hot is cold. If I asked, What's the opposite of fast? the answer would be slow. For dark, the answer would be light; for day, it would be night; for over, under; for a conscious thought, an unconscious thought; and for Yin, Yang. I could fill a thousand pages with examples of *apparent dualities* and barely scratch the surface. Everything has an opposite, and only when we have experienced both sides can we truly know them separately. Then we can use this knowledge to find the balance point in the center, a location that is metaphorically neither too hot nor too cold. For example, through my years of traveling around the world on humanitarian missions, I have been exposed to both extremes regarding accommodations.

In Lima, Peru, our hotel was in the barrios, the poorest section of downtown Lima. It was dark, damp, filthy, and inexpensive, which didn't give me the most secure feeling during my stay. In Dubai, we stayed in the world's only seven-star all-suite hotel, surrounded by excess and opulence. It was bright, dry, spotless, and posh, and even though it was in the Middle East, it filled me with a secure feeling. Those who have only seen one side of the coin have no comparison of the opposite, of the duality between the lavish hotel and the dilapidated flophouse.

This is where personal experience and life exploration come into play. Stepping out of our comfort zones often opens us up to find the balance point between the *apparent dualities*. Only by knowing the positive attributes of the hotel in Dubai could I understand the negative qualities of the hotel in Lima and vice versa. I couldn't make this comparison by only knowing one side. In simpler terms, if you keep your home's thermostat set to fifty degrees, you freeze; if it's at ninety degrees, you roast. But if you find the balance point between two, say seventy-five, your body feels comfortable. That may sound like a simple thing to figure out, but the same process can be applied to most of life's experiences. Balance is the center point between life's extremes; it's where the mind finds enlightenment. It's what Buddha found while meditating under the tree. Balance is living in the moment. It is not the ultimate high nor the ultimate low; it's the line that divides them.

If only life could stay at this perfect level, everything would be bliss. But let's be honest; this is life, and that's just not going to happen. We need to understand that lows follow highs, and highs follow lows. This is the ebb and flow of the universe, the temporary motion that carries all of us. Understanding this will allow our minds to move freely around perfect balance. Denying this universal truth can subject us to the depths of depression or unrealistic belief in the permanence of emotional elevation. We must all come down from the mountaintop at some point, but we don't have to stay at the bottom in its shadow.

Let's look at a perspective from an ancient time

In China's sixth century, a contemporary thinker named Lao Tzu wrote an essential philosophical work called the *Tao Te Ching*, which roughly translates to *The Way and Law of Natural Goodness*. Lao Tzu spoke of *The Way*, which is the force of life that flows throughout the universe, and of the *Ten Thousand Things* which make up all the physical elements of life. Today, in our much more advanced and technology-driven world, we are inundated by things, but in Lao Tzu's time, the concept of ten thousand things must have seemed limitless. It includes not just water, wind, fire, rocks, and items used in everyday life, but people, and anything that would allow a human to be a human. Lao wrote about how humans could best live in the universe's life force while interacting daily with every physical item around us. Mastery of this practice allows us to balance our spiritual side with our physical side: it is an expression of apparent duality. Do we marvel at the distant forest or get awestruck by the complexity of the trees in it? We do both.

As Lao Tzu advised, one must live within *The Way* but remember the *Ten Thousand Things.* In other words, we must live in the present moment while interacting with the physical world around us. While your mind may be enlightened, you must still pay the bills.

Achieving Nirvana/Enlightenment means finding the spot between *The Way* and the *Ten Thousand Things*—the balance point. This can be extremely challenging in today's society of instant Internet gratification, financial hardships, cell phones, and jobs extending past a forty-hour work week. But with practice, it is possible.

From my global humanitarian travels, I have realized that we could all learn a thing or two about balance from our third-world neighbors because they live so much closer to the original *Ten Thousand Things* that Lao Tzu spoke of. Modern technology has increased the number of the *Ten Thousand Things* exponentially, greatly clouding the picture.

Verse fourteen of the Tao Te Ching describes The Way.

Look, it cannot be seen - it is beyond form.
Listen, it cannot be heard - it is beyond sound.
Grasp, it cannot be held - it is intangible.
These three are indefinable;
Therefore they are joined in one.
From above, it is not bright;
From below, it is not dark:
Unbroken thread beyond description.
It returns to nothingness.

The form of the formless,
The image of the imageless,
It is called indefinable and beyond imagination.
Stand before it, and there is no beginning.
Follow it, and there is no end.
Stay with the ancient Tao,
Move with the present.
Knowing the ancient beginning is the essence of The Way.

Here Lao Tzu speaks of the law of universal opposites; we can find balance in avoiding either extreme.

When people see some things as beautiful,
Other things become ugly,
When people see some things as good,
Other things become bad,
Lao Tzu

Shape Clay into a vessel;
It is the space within that makes it useful.
Cut doors and windows for a room;
It is the holes which make it useful.
Therefore, benefit comes from what is there;
Usefulness from what is not there.
Lao Tzu

Find the emptiness
Inside
The center of balance
And let it fill up
With true life.

If you think about winning, you also have to think about losing. Think of neither! Be balanced.

Where does stress come from?

Stress comes from the conflict between two thoughts, two dualities: It comes from having the question but not the answer, which is again being caught between two thoughts. Here your mind can find no balance point.

Addictions, religion, and artists

Enlightenment, true enlightenment, is freedom from thought. Whether or not we admit it, we all seek ways to calm the voices that constantly clamor about the future or regret the past and restore focus on the present

Does our subconscious self so yearn to return to enlightenment and restore our bond with the universal God, that it creates addictions to fill the void?

Addictions

During an alcohol or drug-induced event, our minds seem to find a place in the present, though in an altered state. Nothing else really matters. Future thoughts and past memories are pushed aside. Our attention span and memories are shortened and, much like an infant, we live in the moment and react to things going on around us at that present moment. It is a pale reflection of true enlightenment.

Religion

As in addiction, many find an altered state during religious and other spiritual ceremonies. The brain produces endorphins, creating euphoric feelings. There is usually a single conscious collective at work during the ceremony and participants share the same message or experience, expanding the energy around them. During these spiritual activities, the present moment is all that there is.

Artists

When in a creative state, an artist's mind is so focused on the movements it takes to create the work and to pull in the image they have created that they find balance. They are locked in the present moment. While carving, sculpting, writing, drawing, or painting, we lose track of time; the clock loses its function. The only past we see is what our blank canvas looked like, and our future is the image that will be in front of us when we complete our masterpiece. Here, past and future thoughts bring us to the present actions to help create our artistic works.

Insert 6—The Beginning of My Spiritual Journey

I can't remember exactly how old I was, but I must have been in my early twenties. I was chasing down stunt work and more than likely collecting unemployment from previous jobs. I had a lot of time on my hands and very little on my mind; I was a blank spiritual slate.

One morning, I woke up with the urge to go to the library. I couldn't imagine why. I never read anything in those days and didn't even have a library card. But a strong force pulled me in that direction. So, I just went. I didn't question it or reason with myself; I just got up and drove there. Once inside, I meandered around a bit until I found myself standing in front of the rack containing the library's selection of books on tape. Still not sure what the hell I was doing there, I began to thumb through the plastic binders containing books. I must have made a dozen passes over one book before I finally pulled it from the shelf. I patiently read the title and then flipped the case around to read the description on the back. The book was *Anatomy of The Spirit*, by Carolyn Myss. This was something that I would normally have had no interest in listening to, but it stayed in my hand. Then, strangely, I found myself applying for a library card so I could check the tapes out.

Once done, I sat in my truck for a few minutes, just staring at the title on the cover, before I opened the case and inserted the first tape into my cassette player. I couldn't stop listening; it was astonishing. *Anatomy of The Spirit* explained exactly why I had gotten up off my couch, climbed into my truck, and driven to the library to find this exact book. This was the point at which the universe decided to open my eyes to why we humans are on this earth and what life is essentially all about.

How do I explain this? The book covered many spiritual topics that I found interesting, but the message for me was about moving forward into the unknown, bravely walking into the unfamiliar through the doors that open up in front of you. You let go of where you think you are supposed to be and what you want to do in this life, and let the universe guide you in the moment, without question. Carolyn said that we really can't make a wrong decision in these situations, because God, or the universe, if you prefer, doesn't need our help to plan our lives.

In one chapter, she told a story of a gentleman who worked for a limousine company. One day, when he had the limo parked at his house, a group of neighborhood children asked him if they could have a ride. Reluctantly, he finally said, "Fine, you can all have a ride, but you have to ask for your parents' permission first." The children did and, before long, he had a limo full of happily laughing kids and even a couple of parents too.

The man had no idea why he said yes to the wishes of the children. This was an uncharacteristic thing for him to do and, at first, he kept thinking, "What am I doing?" After a short time though, he began to find the children and the ride enjoyable. Sometime later, when he had saved enough to buy his own limousine, he decided to throw caution to the wind and open his very own limo service. The father of one of the children to whom he had given a ride that day turned out to be a highly paid executive for a major corporation. Remembering the man's generosity to the neighborhood kids, he hired the new limo service and recommended it to some of his other highly paid business associates. Within a short time, the man's new limo service was booming with more clients than he ever imagined. The simple act of not saying no to the children who wanted a free ride changed his life.

Open-Heart Love

Love is the bridge between you and everything
Rumi

What is open-heart love?

Open-heart love is a way of loving that comes from a place of emotional honesty, vulnerability, and deep presence. It is love that flows freely—without fear, control, or barriers. When someone loves with an open heart, they are emotionally available—willing to feel, connect, and share without shutting down. They are vulnerable and non-possessive—not afraid to be seen as they are, imperfections and all. They love without trying to own, change, or limit the other person.

They are compassionate, courageous, and present—empathy, kindness, and patience reside at their core. They love even when it's scary, uncertain, or painful, and they're not stuck in the past or afraid of the future; they embrace love in the present moment.

Open-heart love is not a gentle or passive, either. It is powerful because it doesn't hide. Loving with an open heart doesn't mean allowing people to walk all over you or disregarding boundaries. It means showing up authentically, loving without defenses, and creating space for connection, even when it's uncomfortable.

Where in the body does love originate?

The experience of love is profoundly human. Although we often perceive it as solely emotional or spiritual, it has real roots in both the brain and body. It represents a beautiful dance between biology, emotion, and consciousness.

The brain is the command center of love.

The limbic system, often referred to as the emotional brain, particularly involves the amygdala and hippocampus. It plays a crucial role in processing emotional experiences and linking memories to love and is why a specific song evokes thoughts of someone you care for. The hypothalamus triggers the release of bonding chemicals like oxytocin and dopamine, which generate feelings of pleasure, connection, and trust. Meanwhile, the prefrontal cortex is responsible for decision-making and long-term thinking. In the context of love, it aids in attachment, empathy, and envisioning a future with someone.

The human body produces love chemicals, some of which we've encountered previously. These chemicals serve as the body's language of connection. Oxytocin is the bonding hormone; it's released through touch, eye contact, and trust, intimacy, and it strengthens feelings of closeness in romantic, familial, and platonic love. Dopamine is the pleasure and reward chemical; it creates feelings of joy, excitement, and infatuation, driving the desire and passion associated with love. Serotonin, endorphins, and vasopressin all play roles in emotional balance, bonding, and the long-term maintenance of love.

The heart (yes, quite literally)

Though we symbolically say "love comes from the heart," the heart and brain are actually in constant communication. Your heart rate changes with emotional states, especially love. Heart rhythms become more coherent and harmonious during feelings of love, gratitude, and connection.

The soul or consciousness (the spiritual origin)

People also experience love as a soul-level energy, a force that transcends the physical realm. In spiritual traditions, love is often regarded as the essence of life itself or even as the divine expressing itself through us. This deeper form of love doesn't rely on hormones; it is eternal, expansive, and unconditional.

The sense of love is a beautiful union that combines the biological chemistry of your brain and nervous systems, the emotions in your heart and memory, and your soul's longing to connect, give, and be known. All of this melds together to create the spiritual self.

How does love affect our health?

Love profoundly impacts our health; it has the power to heal us. Yet, when it is distorted or lost, it can also bring pain. It is one of the few human experiences that affect us physically, emotionally, mentally, and spiritually all at once.

The positive effects of love

People in loving relationships—romantic or not—tend to live longer. Love lowers blood pressure, supports heart health, and enhances immune function. Affectionate touch, connection, and support diminish cortisol (the stress hormone). Cuddling or simply feeling emotionally safe boosts oxytocin, soothing the nervous system.

Studies indicate that people recover more quickly from injury or surgery when surrounded by love and support. Emotional support enhances immune responses and reduces inflammation. Love improves mood, resilience, and self-worth. It can alleviate symptoms of anxiety, depression, and loneliness. Loving connections provide individuals with a sense of meaning and belonging. Both physical and emotional love—especially through touch—can diminish physical pain. The brain even releases natural painkillers (endorphins) in the presence of love.

The negative effects of love

Emotional pain from loss, rejection, or betrayal can activate the same neural pathways as physical pain. Broken heart syndrome is real—it can cause chest pain and, in rare cases, heart dysfunction. Chronic stress from abusive or unhealthy relationships increases cortisol levels, leading to weight gain, inflammation, insomnia, anxiety, and even heart disease. When love turns into fear or control, it becomes emotionally and physically draining.

When it turns into attachment or obsession, love can create cycles of addictive behavior, withdrawal symptoms, and unstable mental health. Profound love can lead to profound grief, which may weaken the immune system, disrupt sleep, and impact long-term mental and physical health.

Healing love. It's all about the balance

When love is healthy, it's one of the most profound medicines we have. However, when it's wounded, it can cut just as deeply. The key is to cultivate love that is mutual, compassionate, and rooted in respect. It must be balanced between giving and receiving, while also being spacious enough to allow for freedom, not control. This is why so many people find volunteer work, philanthropy, mission work, or an altruistic lifestyle so appealing. Love is God's free medicine.

Love is the central message of nearly all of the world's religions and spiritual beliefs. In yogic and spiritual traditions, the heart chakra, known in Sanskrit as Anahata, is the fourth energy center in the body. It serves as the bridge between the lower three chakras (related to survival, sexuality, and power) and the upper three (connected to insight, intuition, and divine consciousness).

The heart chakra is located in the center of the chest, near the heart. It is associated with the color green and the element of air, possibly because humans cannot live without both air and love. It governs love (both giving and receiving), compassion (for yourself and others), forgiveness (letting go of pain and resentment), connection (to people, nature, and the universe), balance (emotional harmony and inner peace), and healing (both emotional and energetic).

When your heart chakra is balanced, you are open to love, compassion, and acceptance. You feel emotionally centered, grateful, able to forgive, and connected to life. Conversely, the opposite—*apparent dualities*—can hold true when our heart chakra is blocked or out of balance. This may manifest as difficulty in trusting or forming deep connections, leading to fear of intimacy, jealousy, bitterness, or resentment. It can cause us to hold onto past heartbreak, resulting in emotional numbness or isolation. The heart chakra is where the soul speaks softly. When it's open, we see through the eyes of love—not just romantic love, but the love that honors all life.

In the Christian faith, love is the very heart of Jesus' message and arguably the deepest thread running through his life, teachings, and presence. It is not a soft or sentimental kind of love, but a radical, world-shifting, unconditional love that calls people into wholeness, compassion, and connection. Jesus didn't just speak of love—he commanded it:

> *"Love the Lord your God with all your heart, soul, mind, and strength… and love your neighbor as yourself."*
> Mark 12:30–31

These two commandments sum up the entire law and the prophets. For Jesus, love was the measure of all things, love without borders—*open-heart love.* He loved the poor and the outcast, the sinner and the saint, women, children, lepers, and even his enemies, including those who would betray or kill him. His love shattered barriers of class, religion, gender, and purity. That kind of love isn't easy. It's divine. For Jesus, love wasn't just a feeling but a way of being, and can be found throughout the gospels.

> *"Love your enemies, do good to those who hate you."*
> Luke 6:27

> *"Greater love has no one than this: to lay down one's life for one's friends."*
> John 15:13

"By this everyone will know that you are my disciples, if you love one another."
John 13:35

Jesus didn't leave behind wealth or a political system—he left behind a way of love. The kind of love Jesus embodied isn't transactional; it's transformational. It invites you into union with God, the universe, compassion, and humanity. It's self-emptying love (kenosis)—a giving of oneself fully, freely, and without condition. That love is still alive, still unfolding, still calling out to those of us ready to accept it.

Talking to strangers

In our fast-paced, digitally connected world, the idea of striking up a conversation with a stranger might seem daunting or even outdated. We often stick to the comfort of our existing social circles, both online and offline. However, there is a profound and often underestimated humanity in engaging with strangers. These seemingly random interactions can significantly impact our lives and the world.

Talking to strangers can open up new worlds and expand our horizons. Each individual carries a unique perspective and life experience. Engaging in conversation with people you've never met can introduce you to diverse cultures, beliefs, and lifestyles. These interactions can challenge your preconceived notions and expand your worldview. You might learn about a new hobby, a cultural tradition, or a personal life story that profoundly impacts your outlook.

We live in a diverse world, yet it is easy to become isolated within our social bubbles. Engaging in conversation with strangers allows us to bridge these gaps, fostering empathy and understanding. Through dialogue, we can learn about the challenges and triumphs faced by people from all walks of life. This firsthand understanding builds empathy and promotes inclusivity. It serves as a reminder that we share the same human experience, regardless of our differences.

Every interaction with a stranger is an opportunity to create a positive impact. A simple smile, a friendly greeting, or a supportive conversation can make someone's day. We often underestimate the power of these small gestures. They can lift spirits, combat loneliness, and remind people that they are not alone in this world. Acts of kindness toward strangers help strengthen the bonds that hold our society together; they can also create serendipity and opportunities.

Some of life's most meaningful moments result from chance encounters. Whether you are meeting a potential business partner, finding your soulmate, or stumbling upon your dream job, luck often plays a significant role. Engaging with strangers creates opportunities for these chance encounters. By talking to people outside your usual circle, you increase the odds of serendipitous moments that can change your life.

Talking to strangers is not just about individual connections; it contributes to a greater sense of community. The more we engage with others, the stronger our social fabric becomes. Communities are built on relationships, and these relationships begin with conversations. Talking to strangers creates a more inclusive and connected world where people feel seen and heard. The fear of the unknown often leads to prejudice and discrimination. Talking to strangers can break down these barriers. When we humanize those we perceive as "others," it becomes harder to hold onto stereotypes and biases. Personal connections disrupt the dehumanizing effects of discrimination and can force social change.

The humanity of talking to strangers is rooted in our innate desire for connection and understanding. These interactions can expand our horizons, cultivate empathy, create meaningful moments, and foster a stronger sense of community. By embracing the art of conversation with those we've never met, we can enrich our lives and contribute to a more compassionate and interconnected world. So, don't be afraid to start a conversation with a stranger; you may be surprised by the profound impact it can have on your life and the lives of others.

Insert 7—Culture Shock in Guwahati, India

Culture shock in any developing country can take you by surprise, but India, with the world's largest population, is a monster all its own. Add to that the fact that we were in a location so remote that even people who live in India's larger cities never see it, and you get mega culture shock.

People were everywhere and there were numerous soldiers in the streets. Guwahati is in Assam Province, which was governed by the military. Rumor had it that the province wanted to secede from India and become its own country. We were told that, because of the high military presence, the streets were extremely safe; the men with guns were there to influence locals, not to engage in violent acts upon each other, and, especially, not toward any tourists who might venture away from their hotels to explore the street life.

Of the many contrasts of culture I experienced, I believe the hardest for me to get used to was the Indian peoples' lack of personal space. Maybe it's because of the hordes of people inhabiting the country, or maybe it's just that we in the United States over-value our spatial distance from other bodies. I'm not sure. What I do know is when you get in a conversation with a person in Assam Province, expect a lot of head bobbling and almost nose to nose contact as they speak to you. To an outsider, it can be quite awkward when a stranger comes in so close to talk that you start to wonder if he's going to kiss you on the mouth. Of course, as you start to back away from the conversation, they keep moving forward until you either get pinned against a wall or trip over something.

My personal fun experience with this happened during an event thrown for the volunteer doctors on our mission by the Ministry of Health of Assam Province. This Operation Smile mission was a huge deal to the region; no other group of volunteers had ever come to Guwahati before. So the entire team was treated with much love and respect, even John and me. Preceding this grand event of chanting, dancing, and ceremonial activities, the Minister's special security team came out to conduct a thorough bomb search. John and I clued into what was going on when an old mama Doberman Pinscher with six saggy teats walked past and sniffed the couch on which we were comfortably resting. In an extremely polite tone, the dog's handler looked at us and asked if we would please stand for a moment. To our surprise, a second man, garbed in all black, ran a small metal detector over the cushions we had been sitting on and then lifted the front of the couch to perform the search on the underside.

"It's OK," he said, and he gave us a thumbs up and a goofy smile before following the aging dog to another couch to check. As I stood there, laughing to myself at the idea that I just been sitting on a couch rigged to blow up, another man approached me. He was dressed in an all-black suit, and it was obvious that he had something to do with the security operation at hand. He was tall, with very dark skin; his hair was jet black and well groomed; and he had a moustache that would make even the Mario brothers envious. I looked over and cordially acknowledged his approach with a friendly smile and a nod. The man seemed very focused on me; he just kept coming closer and closer until his moustache hovered inches from right cheek bone. Talk about feeling uneasy.

"Are you enjoying yourself in our country?" He had a thick Indian accent, with a strong vibrato. This was followed with, "Is this your first time in India?" To my relief, he was just making small talk, trying to be friendly to a visiting volunteer.

Universal Karma

Karma is the destiny man weaves for himself.
L. H. Leslie-Smith

Universal karma refers to the principle that all actions—whether by individuals, communities, or humanity as a whole—have consequences that ripple through the interconnected web of life. It's not just personal karma ("what goes around comes around" for me), but also the understanding that everything is connected and that our actions contribute to a larger cosmic balance.

What is karma?

In Sanskrit, karma means "action" or "deed." It represents the law of cause and effect. Every thought, word, or action sows a seed, which ultimately bears fruit—whether in this life, another life, or collectively across time.

So, universal karma is the understanding that karma doesn't just apply to individuals; it also applies to families, cultures, nations, and even the planet. Every choice made by a person or group affects the whole. We're not isolated beings; we're part of a living, breathing whole.

Think of it like an ocean: one drop causes ripples that touch every shore. Universal karma reminds us that everything is sacred and our choices matter—far beyond what we can immediately see. It invites us to live with integrity, compassion, and a sense of responsibility for the collective good. It's the natural unfolding of energy. What I do to you, I also do to myself, and vice versa. These patterns repeat until the energy is transformed through awareness and love. It's collective healing; justice and compassion ripple outward, lifting communities and future generations.

In short, universal karma is a quiet, cosmic mirror. It doesn't judge—it reflects. It asks, *"What are we creating together? And how can we choose better, more loving seeds to plant in the world?"*

The power of inner knowing

Human intuition is the ability to understand or know something instantly, without needing conscious reasoning. It's often described as a "gut feeling" or an inner sense that guides decisions or judgments, particularly in complex or uncertain situations. As humans beings, we know right from wrong. We have an inherent ability to recognize those who have needs, those without, and those who are suffering. These are the feelings that keep us up at night or cause us to return to the corner store to buy a homeless stranger a hot cup of coffee on a cold, rainy night.

Intuition operates quickly and effortlessly. It's the mind's way of making fast judgments based on prior experiences, patterns, and emotional signals. It is deeply connected to pattern recognition. The brain subconsciously scans past experiences and environmental cues to draw conclusions or anticipate outcomes.

Intuition sharpens with experience. Experts in a field often make intuitive decisions that seem immediate but are actually grounded in years of learning and exposure. Emotions frequently play a key role in intuition. The body may react physically (e.g., a tight chest or sense of ease) based on subconscious emotional assessments.

Psychologist Daniel Kahneman described intuition as part of "System 1" thinking—fast, instinctive, and emotional—as opposed to

"System 2," which is slower, deliberate, and logical. While powerful, intuition isn't infallible. It can be influenced by biases, stereotypes, and incomplete information, which may lead to poor judgments if not balanced by reasoning.

In essence, intuition is the mind's quick path to navigating the world, often merging knowledge, emotion, and subconscious processing.

For example, a seasoned firefighter enters a burning house and suddenly shouts for his team to get out—just moments before the floor collapses. He can't explain exactly why he knew danger was imminent, but his years of experience triggered subtle cues: the heat felt too intense, the silence too complete, or the fire's behavior slightly abnormal. This is intuitive expertise at work—his brain recognized a dangerous pattern without needing conscious analysis.

Neuroscience shows that the brain processes much more information than we are consciously aware of. The basal ganglia and anterior cingulate cortex play a role in intuitive decision-making. Studies using brain imaging techniques, such as fMRI, reveal that people often make decisions before they become consciously aware of them—suggesting that intuition first operates at a subconscious level.

Psychologists like Gary Klein (with his "Recognition-Primed Decision" model) have studied how professionals—military leaders, nurses, and pilots—use intuition to make high-stakes decisions effectively. These aren't wild guesses; they are fast assessments based on pattern recognition and emotional memory.

The more you immerse yourself in a field (e.g., writing, teaching, leadership, medicine), the more your brain constructs a rich library of patterns and cues. Intuition sharpens with context.

Meditation, quiet reflection, or simply disconnecting from constant input—such as phones or noise—helps you hear your inner voice.

Intuition often speaks in calm, subtle signals; silence allows them to surface.

Journal and reflect on your decisions; write down the choices you made based on gut feelings. Later, evaluate the outcomes. This builds a conscious link between instinct and results, refining your intuitive accuracy. You might notice emotional cues as your body reacts to subtle information. Pay attention to how you feel physically when something "feels off" or "feels right"—tight shoulders, calm breathing, etc. Learn to test your intuition in low-risk situations to build confidence. Over time, trust grows—but pair it with logic when the stakes are high.

Insert 8—Karma and Clint Eastwood

In the beginning of my humanitarian journey, I coordinated my first trip to Carmel with Mia Hamwey. "Before you come out here," she said, "there is one person that I want you to speak with on the phone. Her name is Dina Eastwood." I paused. "Eastwood?" I asked. "As in Clint Eastwood's wife?" "Yes," Mia said, "She is a dear friend."

Like most stunt guys, I am a huge fan of Clint Eastwood and his movies. Now I was instructed to call his house and ask to speak to his wife. It took about two weeks to make this phone call happen and I was on a vacation, in Las Vegas of all places. On the appointed day, I anxiously sat in my room waiting for two o'clock, the agreed upon time for my call. Then, palms sweating, I picked up my phone and dialed the number that Mia had given me. A female voice answered,

"Hello, this is Dina."

"Hi, Dina, it's Kevin Ball." There is a long pause, followed by an almost frantic voice that caught me a bit off guard.

"Oh my God, Kevin. I dropped my laptop and I don't know what to do. It has all my family photos and work on it." The urgency in her was so down to earth that it reminded me of the recurring tech talks I had with my own mother. My heart rate steadied and I went into help mode.

"What type of laptop is it?"

"It's a Mac," she said. That was our connecting point, the simple word "Mac." I calmed her down a bit, told her the information on the hard drive was fine, and advised her to take it to the local Apple store where they could retrieve everything. I totally forgot I had called to talk to her about filming a documentary on her group until she said, "I get a good feeling about you, Kevin, and I think it's great that you want to help out the group. I can't wait to meet you in Carmel when you come to visit us next month." That was it; no stress and not the Spanish Inquisition that I was expecting.

After I returned home, I pushed the trip on John again and told him that Mia and I had set a date for me to fly out and meet the group. I filled him in on the amazing phone call with Dina Eastwood, and how the documentary idea was moving forward.

About a week later, John hit his maximum stress level at work. I pulled him away from his duties to help me move some tractors that were used to tow parade floats. It was brainless, almost relaxing, work and John needed to relax. So, it was perfect.

As a few of the tractors were broken down and would not run under their own power, we decided to use a rope and tow them around the perimeter road that encircled the park. John steered the nonworking ones as I drove the tractor towing him.

In that moment John let go of what he thought he was supposed to do and let the universe take over and guide his direction. As I was pulling him down the back roads of the park he started to smile, then he started to laugh, and then he yelled, "I am having fun right now! I just had an epiphany: I hate my job! I am coming to Cambodia with you to film this thing!"

So, fate, karma, and stress forged our new filming partnership. We named it Karma180 Productions. People always ask, "Why didn't you name it Karma 360? That would be a full circle and things would come back to you." My response is that this is not the way karma works. You can't give something away with the hope of getting something back in return. That's not karma: that's greed, and it's the worst type of greed because it's disguised as a favor or a kind gesture. For karma to be true karma you must give away at 180 degrees, not wanting anything back in return. This is the only way to find true karma.

Humanity is not about helping all of the suffering in the world.
Humanity is simply one hand reaching out to help another hand in need.

SECTION III

MY SECOND AWAKENING

My Second Awakening to Humanity and John's Retreat

It was August 2011, and we found ourselves in Brazil. The NGO Operation Smile had asked John and me to see if we were interested in documenting a mission to a small town outside Rio de Janeiro. That was one stamp still missing from our passports, so, as usual, we jumped at the chance to travel to a place that was new to us.

Our contact at Op-Smile informed us that we had been personally requested to document another segment for the organization's annual fundraiser gala, which takes place each year in Los Angeles. During this mission, we were assigned to follow Jennifer Salke and her son, Henry. Jennifer had recently been promoted to president of entertainment at NBC Universal and had a personal interest in Operation Smile because her son, Henry, had been born with a facial cleft nearly ten years earlier. Given her similar story and deep understanding of the challenges faced by individuals with facial deformities, Jennifer and Henry's presentation at the gala would attract considerable attention in Hollywood circles and, hopefully, help raise substantial donations.

We were also asked to film a short piece for Colgate, a major corporate sponsor, conduct some interviews with the newly crowned Miss Brazil, and, as usual, capture shots from all aspects of the mission for archiving purposes. Our plate was quite full. Once again, we discovered another direct correlation between Hollywood and humanity.

Our great friend and mentor, Mark Asher, would join us as the lead photographer, and we were assigned a young lady new to traveling in developing countries as our "lead," so to speak. Her name was Jessica, and among other annoyances—of which there were many—she never figured out which end of our lenses to avoid. Whether it was still camera or video, she would always end up directly in our frame, wildly waving her hands and pointing at the children she thought should be filmed. It was a never-ending battle. After three days, we began heading out early, leaving her at our humble hotel while we found our own ride to the hospital and surgical locations.

Jessica would not be the only new woman to enter my life during this humanitarian mission to Brazil; there was another—one who inspired me to explore new realms to seek those in need, but who also affected me in ways that caused me to follow her around like a cat in heat.

The Woman

When we chose seats at large round tables, like the ones you'd find at a wedding reception, John and I selected a location in a far corner of the room, with our backs to the wall and near an exit. We had adopted this practice from two British Secret Air Service gents who had accompanied us as private security on a mission to Kosovo several years earlier. It gave us a good view of the room, insight into who was coming in and out of the main doors, and early warning of any good moments to document an impromptu speech from one of the Op-Smile team. In some locations, it also provided a few extra seconds to get our asses out of the room if any not-so-polite individuals entered with plans to do no good. It happens.

We had only been in the country for a few days and were attending the traditional meeting to get to know other members of the medical and surgical team. Any Operation Smile mission includes volunteers from across the globe, and it is paramount to get to know the people you will literally be rubbing elbows with around the surgical table. Since this was a mission to Brazil, Portuguese was the primary language spoken in the room, with what sounded to me like a lot of Spanish and bits of German and Dutch thrown in to spice things up. I didn't understand a word, but it was clear that, like in many cultures, the loudest person in the conversation had the floor to speak. As most of the Brazilian medical team were women, there was also what I dubbed a stereophonic cacophony of cackling (I like alliteration) going on.

As usual, our reputation seemed to have preceded us. Although we enter a mission with very little knowledge of the volunteers, many volunteers immediately recognize Kevin and John—the two American stuntmen turned humanitarian video guys. We certainly stand out a bit. During the van ride from the hotel to the lunch location, amidst a barrage of questions, it came out that we had just come from Louisiana, where we were doing stunts for the feature film *Jonah Hex*. Consequently, quite a bit of the Portuguese banter and attention was directed at our table, which consisted of just the two of us at that moment. However, that was about to change. Several things were set to shift as *universal doors* opened for me once again.

Even the screenwriters of black-and-white romantic comedies from times gone by could not have done justice to the scene that was about to unfold in front of John and me.

The afternoon lunch was in its early stages when she walked through the door, late, looking slightly disheveled from her long journey, and breathtaking. We couldn't take our eyes off her. Her gaze was downward as she entered, moving slowly and quietly around the outer perimeter to avoid drawing attention to her arrival. John cleared his throat and gave me the universal guy expression for, "Did you see what just walked through the door?" I acknowledged his look with a short grunt and a quick raise of my right eyebrow, but I was fully aware of the alluring woman. Shoulder-length, dirty blond hair framed her face, the centerpiece of which was the most beautiful pair of full lips. They seemed reluctant to fully close, leaving just enough space to reveal her front teeth—think cute bunny rabbit. Not to be overshadowed were her blue eyes, which appeared even larger and bluer as they were magnified by a pair of black horn-rimmed glasses. To a hot-blooded male, she embodied the international look of the sexy librarian, a common fantasy image any angst-ridden teenage boy would recognize.

I immediately lost interest in the food in front of me as she quietly walked around the room, her sheer dress flowing with each step, surveying the situation and seeking out the most comfortable table to avoid any open ridicule for her tardiness. I must have been staring a hole right through her because she locked onto my eyes like radar and began making her way directly toward our outcast table for two.

I can only imagine that John and I looked like two fourteen-year-old prepubescent boys who had just seen their first boob. Our eyes fixed on her, an expression of both fear and excitement on our faces. It's something that most men never outgrow. When she finally reached our table, we were still in stupid mode, and I don't believe either of us even stood up to greet her. She placed her bag on one of the vacant chairs, pulled out the one in front of her, sat down, and scooted her chair into a comfortable eating position.

Since neither John nor I had said anything, she may have assumed that we did we not speak English but, after what must have seemed like a long moment of silence, she broke the ice first. *"Hi boys, I'm Eva; y'all don't look like locals,"* came out of her mouth in the cutest southern drawl. I melted. With another dramatic pause and still captivated by her beautiful blue eyes, I snapped out of it and introduced myself. John did the same. I was instantly attracted to her. This was not just a simple "I think you're hot" attraction, but a deep, soul connection. There was something special about this woman. What I didn't realize was that Eva was experiencing a similar connection. I didn't purposely ignore John from that moment until the end of lunch, but that's essentially what happened. Eva and I couldn't stop talking, laughing, and discovering everything we could about each other.

As we walked to the van after the luncheon, John looked at me with a touch of dismay and asked, "How?" I simply shrugged my shoulders and smiled. "How and why does this always happen to you?" he repeated. Then, as if I hadn't been at the luncheon, he recounted the afternoon's events to me. "You and I are sitting at a table by ourselves in a foreign country, and the hottest nurse on the mission just walks in and nearly throws herself all over you." I glanced back at him while we walked and said, "I didn't do anything; I was just sitting there." Cutting me off, John said, "That's the thing, you don't ever have to do anything! It just happens to you; how?"

I have never delved deeply into the details of my personality in my writings. I have always relied on stories, adventures, and lessons learned to propel my words forward. Since this book is a bit more candid, I will be as well. *Me*: I have always been somewhat of a ladies' man, especially in my middle years. A professional Hollywood stuntman turned international humanitarian, I bounce around the globe, carrying babies into surgeries, chasing adventure, and laughing calmly through dangerous events. I've been told time and again that I embody the Bad Boy image. Women want to be with a bad boy, and men want to be one. Doctors, dentists, politicians, and even a politician's husband have told me they have a Man Crush on me. This is not a homosexual reference at all; it's a fully respected man-to-man compliment.

I grew up around danger-seeking stuntmen and women, learning to keep a level head in bad situations. The rejections I faced from ruthless casting directors, especially early on, taught me how to talk to anyone without fear of rejection. Moreover, I've always had to keep my body in shape to stunt double for leading male actors, and thanks to some great genes—thanks, Mom and Dad—I've managed to age gracefully with a rugged appeal. I'm not being braggadocious; I'm being a realist. Realistic self-assessment is a critical skill for stuntmen.

I have also spent years honing myself, quietly observing others in deep conversations and daily activities. Life itself can be the best teacher if you take it all in, process it, and rid yourself of actions and thoughts that are self-destructive, negative, and downright unusable for personal growth. I read many books on a variety of topics, watch documentaries, and listen to podcasts; I have always been and still am a sponge for knowledge. These things are why I stand out when I walk into a room. People have an inherent ability to recognize when they meet someone confident and trustworthy—someone they would feel safe following. I am the proverbial Boy Scout, just cocky enough to balance out the confidence. That's why Eva sat at our table.

Let's face it, international humanitarian missions, especially those with an element of danger, can be hookup zones. You are away from friends and family for a couple of weeks, sometimes on the other side of the globe, and with like-minded individuals you may never see again, That you are also caught up in intense human experience adds fuel to an equation that works. I want to clarify, on the record, that nothing serious ever happened between Eva and me. I had a girlfriend at the time, and she was married. John and I shared a small room as our home base, and our work schedules, along with Eva's, usually kept us in different locations throughout the long days of surgery week. But had circumstances been a bit different, who knows what the outcome might have been.

As it turned out, Eva lived in Jacksonville, Florida, my home state. She was a surgical nurse and had participated in as many Op-Smile missions as John and I had, so we were all familiar with the experiences and adventures of humanitarian travel. As the mission progressed, so did my efforts to keep pace with Eva.

John, Mark, and I worked to cross off items on our lengthy punch list. We tagged along with Jennifer and her son Henry, capturing as much footage as we could to edit into an excellent piece for the gala. We secured some compelling emotional interviews with Miss Brazil and Miss Mexico, discovered wonderful faces for the Colgate campaign, and received permission from a local drug kingpin to enter his favela (Brazilian shanty town), documenting the home of a small boy who had undergone cleft lip surgery with us the day before. We even set out on a day trek into the surrounding jungle and countryside to find a couple of children who had undergone surgeries years earlier for updated stories on how their lives had changed.

Everything was going well until Jessica keenly directed our driver on a wild goose chase that left us in a cow pasture in the middle of a random village just as the sun was setting. We quickly retreated as an inquisitive crowd of onlookers approached us, likely wondering why a van full of Americans was trying to avoid getting stuck in a muddy cow pasture so far from the nearest town.

Our mission experiences were always an adventure. In contrast, Eva's schedule was a bit more predictable. She worked in the heart of the surgery ward. Most Op-Smile missions aim for a full five days of surgery. Each day includes up to seven surgical teams, give or take, performing an average of five surgeries lasting one to two hours each. Completing thirty-five children's facial and palate surgeries daily for five consecutive days is no small feat, but they accomplish it, mission after mission. And they do it safely.

I kept track of Eva's whereabouts each day and did my best to drop in for a visit and a quick bit of insider talk about how the teams were holding up and if there were any interesting cases we should know about. It's always beneficial to have someone on the inside to help us journal the mission as it progresses. It also allowed me to exchange closer eye contact with my sexy librarian-bunny-nurse-spy. Her list of pet names kept growing.

The night after the last day of surgeries, John, Eva, and I went out for a bit of fun, fueled by Brazil's local drink, the Caipirinha. This national drink is made with a rum known as Cachaca, a bit of simple syrup, and a lot of muddled lime. It's strong and delicious, and after a few, you start to feel a bit prophetic, just as the three of us did that night. Eva and I wanted to save the world, while John's mind seemed to wander elsewhere; something I would learn more about after we returned home. That evening, this touch of prophetic buzz and the understanding others had about my views on humanity caused one of my *self-actuators* to appear once again. A *universal door* was about to open, and I would leap through to discover the mysteries awaiting on the other side.

Haiti a year after the big earthquake

With the Operation Smile mission to Brazil now a couple of weeks behind us, John and I were deep into editing mode, trying to finish the Los Angeles Gala piece about Jenifer and Henry in time for the big event. John was showing signs of burnout, and I could see his passion for the humanitarian work we were doing diminishing.

I had to do much more editing on my own, and I managed all communication with Op-Smile and a few other NGO clients we were assisting. From the very beginning, this mission to engage and support humanity had always my idea, my initiative, my dream. Sure, John benefited greatly from our years of international travel documenting NGOs, but it wasn't his passion; it was mine. Recognizing that this was happening and that I would need to take on even more responsibilities, I told him that I was setting out on a few solo adventures. Surprisingly, he was very open to the idea.

Weeks earlier in Brazil, during our last evening goodbye conversations, Eva had proposed a possible new adventure to me. She asked if I had ever been to Haiti. Haiti!? I had visited many fascinating, below-poverty-line areas, but I must openly admit that Haiti was one of those places I never had the slightest urge to explore. The only thing I knew about Haiti was that it ranked highly in the global percentage of infectious diseases like AIDS, Hepatitis, dysentery, and cholera.

When news outlets covered stories from the region, they often focused on political strife, poverty, and violent protests. Then there was the devastating magnitude seven earthquake, whose epicenter was only fifteen miles from the capital city of Port-au-Prince, killing around 200,000 people. This mega quake struck on Tuesday, January 12, 2010, just over a year and a half after the Operation Smile mission to Brazil, where Eva and I first met. Little did I know then that the quake was what brought her to Haiti in the first place.

Hundreds of medical personnel bravely volunteered to enter the hardest-hit areas of Haiti and assist with rescue and medical efforts, which turned out to be extensive. Eva's background in surgical room nursing made her an ideal fit for a makeshift surgical camp that treated crush victims needing life-saving limb amputations. Let's take a moment to analyze the reality of this horrific situation and the incredible emotional strength that Eva possessed.

January is the coldest month in Haiti. The temperature typically reaches close to 91 degrees, with an average humidity of 74%. This might sound ideal if you live in Minnesota and wish to vacation at a tropical island resort, lounge by a pool with a cocktail, enjoy continuous access to an air-conditioned suite, and take a refreshing shower. However, that wasn't the reality here. Even a thousand graphic horror movie writers couldn't envision what Eva encountered. The outdated power grid had failed and most of the available electricity came from diesel generators. Bathing was next to impossible and clean water was very limited. In addition, medical centers faced aftershocks, insects, heat, and the persistent diseases that have always plagued Haiti—infection rates now worsened by nationwide destruction.

It was Eva's job to assist doctors in the removal of crushed limbs from survivors pulled from the rubble of fallen buildings. The scene in which she was emersed daily was a tableau of pain, death, destruction, piles of cut-off arms and legs, the smell of decaying flesh in the humid air, and more emotional distress than a human mind is supposed to incur.

Learning all this I greatly respected her and realizing there was still so much devastation to document, even a year later, I agreed to accompany her to the island. As I had many times before, I found myself purchasing an airline ticket to a third-world location with no idea what I would encounter upon arrival. This time, I was going alone, or at least without John. I was getting on a plane, flying to Haiti, all for adventure and a beautiful blonde. Talk about the stuntman coming out; I had no idea what I was getting into!

Disasters breed humanity

Never do the seeds of humanity sprout stronger than when a stranger comes forward to help his fellow man during a global disaster. Just watch the news. Every other image in the story is about people who are now being called heroes.

Heroes opening their homes up to strangers, heroes giving their money and personal belongings to strangers, heroes feeling the call to start non-profit organizations, and, as in the Las Vegas mass shooting, heroes willing to risk their own lives running into a hail of gunfire to help strangers make it to safety.

People think less about themselves; they're more patient, more empathic, and they work harder, faster, and longer—pushing themselves through hours of grueling, dangerous conditions. Let's face it: our species behaves better during catastrophic events than we do on a beautiful Sunday afternoon when our lives seem perfect, when we are waiting in line at a grocery store or attending a sporting event. Maybe this is why disasters happen. Perhaps it's one of the universe's closely guarded secrets that a single disaster is that seed needed to grow countless acts of human kindness and love, regardless of race, religion, creed, gender, or status. All I know is that it truly happens, and I've witnessed it happening all around the globe.

Take, for instance, "The Cajun Navy," a self-titled organization which began as a small group of boat owners from Louisiana who came together after Hurricane Katrina and grew into a well-known nationwide NGO: https://www.cajunnavyrelief.com

Their mission statement reads:

"We are a group of volunteers who work tirelessly without pay to provide immediate rescue and relief during natural disasters. Rescue and relief are our way of sharing the South Louisiana cultural tradition

of neighbors helping neighbors with people in need across the United States. By integrating civilian volunteers into the Incident Command Structure, we can act as a force multiplier for agencies responding to disasters."

A force multiplier is something that increases the effect of a force; a factor or combination of factors that gives people the ability to accomplish greater feats than they otherwise could. Or as the Department of Defense defines it, "a capability that, when added to and employed by a combat force, significantly increases the combat potential of that force and thus enhances the probability of successful mission accomplishment."

In layman's terms and in a humanitarian context, a force multiplier is a person or group that helps aid those in need during a natural or manmade disaster. Not only do they provide aid, but they also organize locals and volunteers into a more efficient workforce. This organization helps yield a much larger result during the initial rescue phase and greatly assists with the rebuilding stage.

Another example is Team Rubicon: https://teamrubiconusa.org. Their mission is to provide relief to those affected by disasters or crises, regardless of when or where they strike. By pairing the skills and experiences of military veterans with first responders, medical professionals, and technological solutions, they aim to deliver the greatest service and impact possible. Team Rubicon seeks to offer our veterans three things they often lose after leaving the military: a purpose, gained through disaster relief; community, built by serving alongside others; and identity, from recognizing the impact one individual can make. This is coupled with leadership development and additional opportunities to assist veterans in transitioning from military to civilian life.

When civilians and volunteers are paired up with force-multiplying NGOs, like the ones named above, the results are amazing, and the accomplishments can be profound. People have inherent goodness. Even individuals who might not normally aid strangers or find compassion in their hearts, muster the strength to put their petty differences aside and embrace love. This is the root of humanity and is at the base of the human moral compass.

Moral compass

The concept of the human moral compass is a fascinating and profoundly ingrained aspect of our existence. It serves as our internal guide, helping us distinguish between right and wrong while directing our ethical decisions and actions.

At its core, the human moral compass is an internalized set of principles and values influencing our ethical decision-making. These principles are shaped by a multitude of factors.

Our first introduction to morality often comes from our families. Parents, guardians, and caregivers play a crucial role in instilling early moral values and shaping our sense of right and wrong. Additionally, the society and culture in which we grow up significantly influence our moral compass. Different cultures have varying ethical frameworks, and we tend to adopt the values and ethics of our communities. Life experiences, both positive and negative, can also shape our moral beliefs. For instance, a traumatic event may lead to a heightened sense of empathy, influencing our moral stance.

Humans possess an inherent capacity for empathy, which often serves as the foundation of our moral compass. This ability enables us to understand and connect with the feelings and experiences of others, promoting pro-social behavior. The moral compass begins to develop in early childhood as we start to grasp concepts such as fairness, honesty, and empathy, which lead to compassion.

Psychologists suggest that this development adheres to a general pattern:

- Preconventional Morality (Ages 0-9): During this stage, children's understanding of morality is largely shaped by the outcomes of their actions. They might follow rules to evade punishment or pursue rewards.

- Conventional Morality (Ages 9-20): During this stage, adolescents begin to internalize societal norms and rules, often emphasizing the importance of conformity and seeking approval from authority figures.

- Postconventional Morality (Adulthood): As individuals mature, they may develop their moral code based on abstract principles of justice and empathy. They question societal norms and may prioritize personal ethics over conformity to the majority.

Our moral compass is not static; it evolves over time. Life experiences, exposure to diverse perspectives, and changes in beliefs can all influence the direction of our moral compass. However, core values often remain stable unless there is a significant shift in one's worldview. Moral dilemmas are situations in which our moral values conflict. Our moral compass guides us in these moments, but the conflict can lead to inner turmoil. We may find ourselves weighing the pros and cons, seeking advice, or making tough decisions that prioritize one value over another. It's in these moments that we honestly grapple with our ethical principles.

How can you develop your strong moral compass?

- Self-Reflection: Regularly contemplate your values and beliefs. Consider why you hold certain principles and whether they align with your true self.

- Open-Mindedness: Embrace different perspectives and worldviews. Engaging in conversations with individuals from diverse backgrounds can expand your moral horizons.

- Empathy: Cultivate empathy by striving to understand the experiences and emotions of others. This can help you make more compassionate and ethical decisions.

- Moral Discussions: Engaging in moral discussions and seeking guidance from trusted mentors or advisors can help to refine and strengthen your moral compass.

The human moral compass is a complex and vibrant aspect of our humanity. It is shaped by numerous influences, including our upbringing, culture, personal experiences, and innate empathy. While it evolves, our core moral values often remain stable, serving as a guiding force in our ethical decision-making. Navigating moral dilemmas can be challenging, but through self-reflection, open-mindedness, empathy, and meaningful discussions, we can cultivate and maintain a strong and ethical moral compass that guides us through the complexities of life.

Eva and I met in Miami for the short flight to Haiti; she arrived from Jacksonville while I came from Orlando. Neither of us knew what to expect. We had first met in Brazil a few months earlier, and there was a lot of sexual tension between us. Now here we were. My biggest fear was what I would find in Haiti; hers seemed to be confronting whether she still wanted to do bad things to me, though I believe she used more adult words to convey her feelings.

I found myself drifting into a black-and-white film fantasy from days gone by. I felt like I was Humphrey Bogart in *Casablanca* or Cary Grant in *Charade* as Eva and I chatted during the plane ride. But there were a few more uncomfortable moments of silence on the flight than during our first meeting at the luncheon. Even though we were going down to do good, I think we both felt our actions might lead to, well, carnal explorations. There, I said it.

Toussaint Louverture International is the primary airport serving Port-au-Prince and the surrounding areas. I had imagined that the airport would look almost the same as it did pre-mega-quake; well-used facilities in developing countries seldom receive any upkeep beyond what is essential to get planes on and off the tarmac. This would be no exception. Touchdown on the crumbling runway was successful, or at least well "in God's hands." Eva and I took the stairs down to the hot tarmac and proceeded to the terminal to retrieve our bags.

Entering the airport from the runway and then exiting onto the public streets is like passing through a portal between worlds. Haiti punched me square in the face like no other international location ever has. Even in India, the overcrowded masses of humanity seemed to ebb and flow in some form of a pattern. Haiti was chaos.

The first thing I noticed, as I stood in the pickup/drop-off zone, just beyond the airport doors, was the complete lack of safety. I'm not suggesting there is any real safety in front of an airport in Cambodia, India, or even Nairobi. But at least there is a police or security presence, even if just for show. But here? Nothing. Nothing but very vocal young men, all eager to take you and your bags on a ride to who knows where, resulting in who knows what. Seriously, if you're not extremely—and I do mean extremely—careful, you can easily disappear within moments of stepping onto Haitian soil, never to be heard from again. This is not an exaggeration.

I was a bit taken aback by the scene before me, but Eva, in total control, seemed right at home. She grabbed my hand, looked me in the eyes, and shouted loudly enough that I could hear her over the street noise, "Don't lose sight of me!"

I had no intention of losing sight of her; she was the only human I knew in Haiti. If I lost her, I would have to live in the airport for the next five to ten days because my white butt wasn't going to wander around these streets alone like I had in other countries. And since I had followed the sexy blonde nurse this far, I wanted to see where this little escapade would lead. Thank God she had a plan because, for once in my life, I was flying blind—following instead of leading. That's not a feeling I cherish.

Together, we ventured further away from the safety of the airport's main doors, passing groups of men all too willing to relieve us of our bags and provide a ride. I had no idea where we were going but, as we continued into the parking lot, Eva instructed me to look for a white van—or any vehicle—with the letters HCM printed on the side. HCM, as it turned out, stood for Haitian Christian Mission. This was our contact and destination.

For a time, we wandered through a sea of vehicles parked in no discernible pattern, Eva began to yell "HCM" loudly. The heat was sweltering, the air was thick with the foul aromas of open sewers, and I just knew we were moving in circles. By now I doubted that anyone was coming to get us, but Eva continued to shout "HCM." She laughed as she shouted; still apparently unconcerned.

"Are you looking for Edwens Prophete?" We turned as a young, well-dressed Haitian man approached us from the street. With a look of relief, Eva replied "yes" and gave him a big hug that seemed to catch him off guard. She recognized him from a previous mission trip, but I don't think he remembered Eva. Now blushing, the young man led us to an unmarked white minivan that looked like it had seen its share of off-road excursions and had lost a few battles with roadside guardrails.

Edwens was a native Haitian and the son of Etienne and Betty Prophete, the founders of the Haitian Christian Mission. He differed significantly from most locals I had encountered since our arrival. He dressed very well in contemporary fashions, his skin was a few shades lighter, and his smile could charm a room without him uttering a word. He was pursuing his MBA at Palm Beach Atlantic University and would travel back and forth to Florida for small business consulting. He also mentioned that he and his brother owned a local company that supplied trucks and construction equipment to the townships. Edwens reminded me of a Haitian version of George Clooney, and when he spoke, he stood out just as much as Eva and I did, but the locals all knew him and respected what he and his family were doing at the mission.

Until now, I had still been flying blind about exactly what HCM did. Eva had only said, "Trust me, it's something you must see with your own eyes." I knew there was a free clinic and a small hospital at the facility; that piece of knowledge and Eva batting her big blue eyes at me had been enough to convince me that I needed to be part of this adventure.

Edwens loaded us into the van and so began my first real encounter with Haiti. The HCM compound was located in the small town of

Fond-Parisien, which means Parisian Valley in French. It was situated about twenty-four miles from Port-au-Prince, but the drive took well over an hour and a half due to highway congestion and poor road conditions. The compound was only six miles from the border with the Dominican Republic, a country with no genuine affection for the Haitian people. There were frequent conflicts at the very small border checkpoint dividing the two countries.

Since our mission had no set schedule and we could expect never-ending traffic rush hour, Edwens decided to take us on a tour of Port-au-Prince and the surrounding areas. The devastating quake had occurred just one year before our trip and he wanted to show us the progress made in that time. Hundreds of millions of dollars in global donations were still pouring into the Haitian government, but I was not naïve about disaster zones and developing nations, I observed the expected outcomes under a corrupt government: opulence for the elites and scraps for the poor.

Many buildings still lay in ruins. The roads were mostly clear of debris; some were completely clear, but on many drivers still had to navigate around large pieces of rubble and collapsed structures. Families and businesses occupied some buildings, but many others were too damaged to reenter. Piles of massive concrete and rebar slabs reminded me of giant fallen dominoes. They had collapsed on top of each other in an almost organized fashion.

Countries like Haiti aren't known for sturdy building construction. Unlike in the US, where regulations are enforced, a small bribe to a city official can allow most public structures to pass a makeshift inspection and be built. This arrangement works well until an overloaded second floor collapses onto the first during a large family gathering or, as we have seen all to many times, when the earth decides it's time to shift.

Haitian construction didn't stand a chance when the epicenter of a game-changing quake struck Port-au-Prince like a dart hitting a bullseye in a game of cricket. The magnitude of the damage didn't hit me until we drove past the former Presidential Palace. If you haven't seen it, please look up photos of it. The best way to describe what I saw is to imagine the US Capitol building in Washington, DC, but with the top rotunda section pulled or pushed about twenty feet from its intended location and haphazardly hanging over the ground structure.

Nothing had been done to wall off or repair the palace; it remained as it was, broken in half, reminding the locals that Haiti was a fractured nation. If the palace in rubble wasn't enough to illustrate the state of Haiti a year after the quake, all one needed to do was stand at the palace gates and turn 180 degrees to find the vast tent city that had formed in an unsanctioned location. This year-old shantytown received no support from local or federal agencies; it was established by displaced people with nowhere to go. Within a year, it had developed its own hierarchy, which included a crime syndicate and served as a cesspool for human trafficking and child prostitution.

We stopped to speak with the inhabitants, and two angry young men demanded that we film what they had to say. They were not looking for handouts or to harass us because of our different skin colors; they wanted us to film them in hopes that we could capture their words and anguish so that someone might hear them and make a change. The most poignant words from one of the young men still linger in my thoughts. He said,

> *"It's not right! It's been a year, and no one has ever come to help us; we are living like devils!"*

I later discovered that encampments like this one, some occupied by thousands, were not officially classified as U.N. refugee camps. They were independently formed by individuals who couldn't reach an officially sanctioned camp or who had been turned away due to overcrowding. I had been on the ground in Haiti for less than a day, and I could already see that Haiti was fucked.

With a long drive ahead, we loaded back into the van to head to the mission location while we still had daylight. I was so intrigued by the stories already coming to life that I wanted to stay near the camp and explore a bit more, but Edwens said that wouldn't be a good idea. He informed us that we were already attracting too much attention, which would put us on the radar of the local street gangs. As I would see in the days to come, Haiti was teeming with angry young men using extreme violence as an outlet for their frustrations, justified or not.

Driving through the streets of Haiti left me with more questions with every bump and turn of the road. Traffic was constant, aggressive, congested, and everywhere. On the other hand, traffic lights, stop signs, road signs, lane markers, sidewalks, and asphalt were nearly nonexistent. Mud filled the potholes that pockmarked the roads, making it difficult to determine the depth of each liquid-filled crater. The water, or light gray viscous substance, that coated the gravel roads did not come from the sky; it emerged from the open sewers, mixed with the garbage that lined the sidewalks, festering into a unique aroma that is hard to describe. Putrid and decaying are the best words that come to mind.

Every kid from my hometown who had to walk home from school beside a busy highway recognized the odor of an animal that had been struck by a car and died not far from the sidewalk. This was that same smell, but here it was everywhere, and you couldn't get it out of your nostrils.

Turn by turn, as we navigated our way through the disheveled city streets, I began to notice something peculiar; at least to me, it was peculiar.

Almost every third vehicle we passed appeared to be a white United Nations vehicle. Trucks, vans, jeeps, and even troop carriers were filled entirely with UN police, easily recognizable by their blue helmets. As I soon discovered, dozens of countries sent their troops to Haiti in the mid-1990s to help with a political upheaval that lasted about seven years. After the major earthquake, they were all redeployed to assist with the organization and security of the many sanctioned refugee camps. Even though most of these camps had been downsized and were receiving less aid from international resources, the UN Blue Helmet peacekeeping forces were still stationed there in the thousands.

If you know anything about United Nations soldiers, you understand that their primary role is to observe and report. Yes, they are an organized army equipped with uniformed ranks and wielding modern weaponry from their home countries, but their orders mandate that they only shoot in self-defense. In war-torn regions, especially in several areas on the African continent, they are permitted solely to report the atrocities committed by rebel and terrorist organizations and are not allowed to engage unless fired upon. In Haiti, on the outskirts of Port-au-Prince, their bases are everywhere. The bases are clean and organized, yet after a year, very little has been done to assist the people of Haiti. They seem to spit in the faces of the locals who starve outside their heavily guarded gates and serve more to mock than to uphold peacekeeping efforts.

The farther we drove from larger towns, the more I began to see a different side of this island country, one that I grew to enjoy. Occasionally, the highways became less desperate, surrendering their craters and fissures to smooth asphalt and a center lane line. This lane line served only as a suggestion to the local Tap-tap and bus drivers, but at least it was there, painted in all its yellow glory on the sunbaked, fading black asphalt. The sky opened up and became bluer; the foliage turned greener; and the air felt fresher, helping to clear the city's smells from my sinuses.

To call Haiti a tropical island paradise is hard because it's not anymore, although it once was. The truth is that Haiti is just poor. The people outside the major cities have almost nothing; hell, the people in the major cities also have almost nothing.

However, let's not confuse this type of poor with the kind of poverty that exists on the African continent. Africa faces lengthy seasonal droughts, leaving desert areas where nothing can grow. It has warlords, child soldiers, and radical religious groups that come into your already impoverished village, burn it down, and chop your hands off, leaving you to suffer, die, or be enslaved.

Haiti suffers from poor management. If you pull up a satellite image on Google of the border area between Haiti and the Dominican Republic, you will see something both amazing and extremely disturbing. Even from a satellite image, a distinct visual border is evident; you can see it because that's where all the trees end.

A literal green wall of trees traces the boundary between the Dominican Republic and Haiti. This is partly why there is so much turmoil at the border crossing points. The Dominican Republic boasts some of the most sought-after beach resort locations in the southern hemisphere; they're opulent tropical paradises coveted by the rich and famous. It's crucial to remember that these lovely beaches and tropical vacation areas share the same island with Haiti. The same piece of land, pushed up from the ocean's depths, formed Hispaniola, home to-both of these countries.

The reason for such a distinctive geographical formation between the two countries is tragic but simple. The people of Haiti have deforested much of their land to produce charcoal, particularly in the poorer areas near the border. For many years, charcoal merchants have stripped the trees from this former island paradise to sell to other impoverished locals for cooking fuel.

The problem is that when the land is stripped of trees, nature itself suffers Without shade, water evaporates more quickly, and the land becomes hotter and drier, creating a manmade tropical island desert. The blame cannot rest solely on the people of Haiti; it mainly falls on the government, greed, and, as previously mentioned, the abysmal management of the country.

The average monthly income for a family in the Dominican Republic is estimated at around $777 (US dollars), equating to about $25 a day. In Haiti, located on the same island, the daily income for more than half the population is estimated to be less than $1 (US dollar), potentially reaching $30 a month if they are extremely fortunate. The Dominican Republic has a population of just over ten million, with a poverty rate of 21%. Haiti's population is slightly larger at eleven point five million, but its poverty rate soars to 58%. By comparison, the US has a poverty rate of around 13%, with a population of 340 million and an average monthly income of $5000.

For now, this concludes our brief overview of Haitian economics. Let's return to my journey to the HCM compound, a journey that would continue as I followed the sexy blonde nurse into what might have been my ultimate demise. At this point, I didn't care; the adventure had me by the soul, and a beautiful, headstrong woman had me by the tenderloins. Well, not yet she didn't, but a stuntman can fantasize, can't he?

The drive continued, with road conditions fluctuating between pleasant and something my body found quite the opposite of enjoyable. The only real memory I retained that might aid me with future directions back to the compound was a giant billboard that seemed completely out of place.

Even now, having made multiple trips to the HCM, I still can't recall what the advertisement on the billboard was. But I can say that the enormous billboard, roughly four times larger than those we see along U.S. interstates, stood like a solitary monolith in the dust and gravel beside the cracked highway. It seemed weirdly out of place, but I knew we were only a few short miles from the mission's hospital compound each time I saw it.

Within a few miles of the colossal beacon, the highway abruptly reverted to its prior, poorly maintained state. The wheels of our outmatched vehicle seemed as if they were struggling to stay attached to their fixed positions at the ends of the axles. The shock absorbers, long beyond their life expectancies, did little to soften the pounding of the drive train against the underside of the van's floor. It was loud enough that most of our conversation was replaced by a few choice words and forceful huffs of air escaping from our lungs with each harsh jolt of the road.

From time to time, we would find some relief from the physical abuse on our bodies as we slowed down to navigate around or negotiate our way past barricades of burning tires set across the roads.

These were local shake-down points for malicious young men seeking to take whatever you owned that they didn't possess but desired. Edwens, well-known in this area, was largely immune to their threats, as many recognized him and understood that the free clinic and hospital at the HCM compound were always accessible, even to them, in times of need. No questions asked.

Eva seemed to laugh it off as a mild annoyance, much like one would with a beggar at their local convenience store asking for some spare change. I, on the other hand, nearly wet my nice travel pants each time we encountered one of these spots, engulfed in black smoke from the roadside fires. Eventually, we reached our destination: the HCM compound.

The first thing one notices upon arriving at the compound is the two massive steel doors guarding the entrance from the road. If you didn't know better, you might think this was some maximum-security prison, situated in a location that no one would ever find and housing the world's most criminal masterminds. As we approached the security doors, Edwens honked the van's horn—the universal signal for "let me in." With the assistance of a few young men inside the secured perimeter, the doors began to part, providing us with enough room to drive inside.

To the left, a small guard shack stood just inside the gates. Inside the small shack was a small man, and in the hands of this small man was a very large gun. Having traveled around the globe and spent time in many developing nations, this scene was no real surprise; however, it reinforced in my mind that we were in a location that was far from safe. It was highly suggested to me, in a few nicely chosen words, that I should not let my white ass wander outside the gates without a security guard. In this case, the small man with the big gun.

We drove up to a white, two-story building and parked alongside a couple of other vehicles in a similar condition to ours, which was not great. Haiti consumes vehicles like Cookie Monster consumes cookies. However, the welcome we received was lovely.

Before Edwens could even shift our rickety van into park, an entire village seemed to emerge from everywhere. Men, women, children, old and young, volunteers, and locals swarmed in, welcoming us to the Haitian Christian Mission. Eva, having been there multiple times before, recognized quite a few faces in the rapidly forming crowd, but I felt like the new boyfriend at a Christmas family reunion; I was greeted, hugged, patted, and kissed. Outstretched hands to shake were thrust at me from all directions. I tried to smile and shake them all, but it was a bit overwhelming.

Then, like Moses parting the sea, the matriarch of HCM effortlessly navigated the crowd, wrapped Eva in a huge embrace, took my hand, and led us inside. It is not an exaggeration to say that Wendy seemed out of place in this environment.

I believe Wendy Zehner is a modern-day Mother Teresa. This was my first meeting with her, but it wouldn't be the last. Wendy's role within the HCM compound was essentially that of the matriarch of the facility; she ensured that everyone had a room in which to stay, that enough food was served at meals, and that the schoolchildren knew their Bible verses. But she was also much more! I have filmed her holding the hand of a woman undergoing local anesthesia as a full-term stillborn infant was cut from her womb, and then tearfully praying afterward. I have seen her barter with unscrupulous individuals for sacks of rice at the seedy warehouses near the port and come out victorious. She once led us on an emergency run to a cholera clinic to retrieve IV bags that were crucial in saving the life of a woman found on the steps of the clinic. I believe she could single-handedly defeat a horde of apocalyptic zombies with a stick and a few well-memorized Bible verses.

I'll discuss Wendy and the Haitian Christian Mission later. For now, let's say that Haiti is both enchanting and perilous. If you turn your back for too long, you may not return from the island, and no one will ever find your remains.

Insert 9—The Razor Wire Hospital and Politics in Nairobi

Kenyatta National Hospital in Nairobi was not what I had expected. With its five-story gray concrete walls, guard gates and razor wire fence, it looked more like a maximum-security prison than a hospital. If not for the beautiful trees and flower gardens that covered the hospital grounds it would have been a ridiculously depressing location for health care. As we toured the facility, I could see that even though the overall appearance was of a more modern hospital, it still had a way to go to meet the standards that we see in the states. The operating rooms were much better equipped than the ones we filmed in Vietnam, but they still needed more attention to bring them up to the needs of the Operation Smile doctors. Pieces of the light fixtures over the operating tables were either missing or broken, the walls were in desperate need of paint, the gray terrazzo floor was stained from years of use and the operating rooms looked like they had been built in the 1960s. With exception of a couple newer pieces of medical equipment, nothing had ever been updated. There were two operation theaters that were attached in the middle by a large open hallway. The hallway also acted as a prep and cleanup location with access to the storage area where the Op-Smile equipment was to be kept. Operation Smile missions have a very high success rate, even though the doctors are sometimes performing up to a combined thirty surgeries per day. This is partly because, no matter where in the world the missions are being held, the equipment the doctors train on and use is the same. It's all shipped in from the states. Each doctor, no matter their nationality, can be sent to any mission site in the world and will find the same life monitoring equipment and the same anesthesia machines. Right down to the portable lights, it's always identical equipment. This stops incidents from happening due to the lack of knowledge or faulty medical equipment that might exist at a foreign hospital. The mortality rate on Operation Smile missions is lower than then the average number of deaths during surgery in the United States. That says a lot for the organization and their practices.

John and I took this first day tour as a time to orient ourselves with the layout of the hospital and worked out a game plan for which topics and volunteers to focus on. We wanted to film and upload as many short stories to the Operation Smile website as we could in the eight-day period. The next morning, after breakfast, Op-Smile's Katherine Taylor asked if we would like to bail on the bus and walk to the hospital. Of course, we said yes; walking always adds that element of danger and adventure we love.

The weather in Nairobi was not what I expected. In the mornings it was cold and wet, with a light, annoying drizzle that kept falling until the sun came out. Then it was beautiful and sunny, but not too hot. Luckily, I had learned from my mistakes to always bring a jacket of some type. I was thankful that I remembered this here. The hospital was about a two-mile walk from our hotel and although the streets were dangerous at night, they had a friendly vibe during the daylight hours. Street vendors would set up at the highway corners and sell drinks, candy, and phone cards. People made their way back and forth along the sidewalks smiling and hooting at each other in a happy manner. There is a very large, although very confusing, mass transit system. The grab hold of anything and hang on system was much in use inside, outside and even on top of the buses the locals rode. As we walked past the traffic police, who wore long black trench coats and carried AK-47's, we watched officers harshly shake down taxi drivers for hundreds of dollars just for crossing over a double yellow line at an intersection. These occurrences brought us back to reality; this was not one of the safest locations for a few white Americans to be.

Also unnerving were the random checkpoints along the highways. Drivers were forced to stop their vehicles at crude looking concrete and rebar spiked barricades. Armed men then approached, aiming their automatic rifles at the side of the driver's head and demanding that they pop the trunk and produce papers. They would then either take what they wanted or just let the vehicle pass. With a state police group, a state military group, a governmental military force, and many private security entities, all wearing different uniforms, you never quite knew who you were dealing with. But they all had big machine guns and they seldom smiled at you. In fact, it would have been creepier if they did smile because you never knew just what they are thinking.

The other thing we noticed, as we walked along the streets to the hospital, was the ever-intensifying political situation. Orange party posters were everywhere, and the current president must have purchased half the billboards in Nairobi to post huge photos of his face. It was the kind of photo in which the eyes follow you wherever you go. I don't know if it was meant to inspire confidence or intimidate, but on his face was a sneering smile that seemed to say, "Reelect me or I will eat your family."

Political rally buses would pass us from time to time. They overflowed with angry young men who wielded clubs and machetes and yelled rallying messages over loudspeakers—both trying to drum up supporters and to intimidate those voting for the opponent. They were just looking for an excuse to instigate violence. We drew some strange looks from passersby as we made our way onto the hospital grounds carrying our Pelican cases and holding tight to our camera gear. Mostly, it was harmless curiosity, although once, as John and I were walking toward the hospital entrance and passed a line of people, someone yelled out, "Hey white man!" in a slow, deep register. I can't say that it absolutely scared the shit out of me, but it did send a few chills down the length of my spine. John looked at me and said, "You did hear that, right?" to which I replied, "Yep... Just keep walking." Sometimes when trouble knocks, it's best to leave the door unanswered.

Katherine, John and I made it out safely and were back in the states before the serious political violence started. The airports were shut down and areas of town burned to the ground only two weeks after we left Nairobi, but happily none of our new friends in Kenya were displaced or killed.

Empowerment Over Charity

One of the first lessons I learned when I became involved with global humanitarian missions was about in-country gifting. This means purchasing goods from local markets, shops, and even street vendors instead of transporting gifts all the way from one's home country.

There are several reasons why this makes sense. First, spending US dollars boosts the local economy, and you get more bang for your buck by purchasing from local vendors. During a mission in Ecuador, our contacts at a local NGO that supported orphanages throughout the country told us that a church group in the US had shipped a large box of donated toys. Unfortunately, the toys remained at the customs office because the import fee was over $700, far exceeding the value of the donation. The $700 fee alone could have bought ten times the number of toys sent if they had been purchased from local markets.

Spending in-country creates a ripple effect. Local vendors and shop owners receive many of their goods from local craftsmen, seamstresses, and farmers. The dollars spent make their way deep into the economic structure. This practice also prevents unscrupulous individuals from stealing donations and reselling them for personal gain, or paying exorbitant dock and import taxes, which are often elevated if the local government knows these donations are for boots on the ground NGOs with little international support.

We encountered this issue in Haiti. Two generators were shipped to the Haitian Christian Mission facility as a gift. When Wendy and the HCM team went to the port to retrieve them, the ship's manifest indicated that only one generator had been shipped. This was, of course, a lie. Frustrated, Wendy told me she could have purchased generators in Haiti for half the cost if money had been sent instead of the items.

We live in a world overflowing with good intentions. Countless dollars are donated each year to developing nations—bags of rice, stacks of shoes, and crates of medicine. While these donations bring relief, they rarely provide a solution. They often address symptoms rather than the underlying systems.

Continual monetary donations can create a cycle of temporary solutions that never truly tip the scale toward independence. They can unintentionally teach communities to wait—relying on others instead of unlocking the strength already within them.

But empowerment? Empowerment does something radical. It says, *"You're not broken. You're capable. Let's begin."*

In the world of international aid and philanthropy, the intentions behind giving are often pure: to help, to uplift, and to alleviate suffering. However, as decades of global aid efforts have shown, good intentions do not always yield transformative results. While monetary donations can address immediate needs—food, shelter, medicine—they often fall short of catalyzing long-term change. Empowerment, on the other hand, plants the seeds of self-reliance, innovation, and dignity. It's not a handout; it's a hand up. In the context of developing countries, it is far more powerful and enduring than continual gifting.

Monetary donations certainly have their place. In times of crisis, such as natural disasters, conflicts, and pandemics, these donations are critical. They enable organizations to respond quickly, save lives, and restore order. However, when giving becomes a routine response to poverty, it risks fostering dependency instead of promoting development.

Communities that rely heavily on external aid can lose the incentive and sometimes the ability to create sustainable solutions for themselves. Local economies may weaken, small businesses may be undermined, and traditional skills may erode. Aid becomes a cycle, and people, no matter how intelligent or driven, become trapped in a system where their survival hinges on the generosity of others. Moreover, corruption, mismanagement, and inefficient distribution systems can drain the impact of financial aid. A donation may enter a system with noble goals, but it can be diluted before it reaches those who need it most.

Empowerment changes the equation. It begins by acknowledging the agency, talent, and potential already present within individuals and communities. It asks not, *"What can we give you?"* but rather, *"What can you do with the right tools, knowledge, and support?"*

Education is one of the most powerful tools for empowerment. Teaching a child to read, a woman to code, or a farmer to increase yield through sustainable practices creates ripples that last for generations. These skills do not depreciate; they grow, evolve, and become the foundation for new opportunities.

Microfinance and social entrepreneurship demonstrate how small investments in people can yield significant returns. When a woman in a rural village receives a microloan to start a small weaving business, she not only lifts her family out of poverty but also contributes to the local economy, hires neighbors, and educates her children. Her success becomes a model for others, and her voice grows stronger in her community. That is empowerment at work.

At the heart of empowerment lies dignity. Monetary aid, especially when offered without context or engagement, can inadvertently imply that the recipient is unable to address their own challenges. Empowerment reverses that narrative. It asserts, *"You are capable. You have value. You are the solution."*

Ownership of progress is crucial. When people engage in their own upliftment, they protect it, sustain it, and pass it on. Schools built with local labor are more likely to be maintained, and water projects led by local committees are more likely to endure. Empowerment is not just about results—it's about who owns the process and who carries it forward.

To empower means transitioning from the role of donor to that of partner. It requires humility and active listening. It asks outsiders to trust that those closest to the challenges often have the clearest insights into the solutions. It necessitates investment not only in projects but also in people—in their ideas, their leadership, and their capacity to lead change. This shift also challenges traditional metrics of success in aid. It's not about how much was given but about how many lives were transformed.

It's not just about numbers; it's about the quality of change—change that is driven by the community and rooted in resilience.

Actual progress in developing countries will not arise from endless streams of donations but from unleashing human potential. Empowerment creates a multiplier effect that fosters independence, innovation, and dignity. It builds communities that are not just surviving but thriving—communities that can, in time, lift others as they have lifted themselves.

By shifting our focus from charity to empowerment, we honor the intelligence, ambition, and dreams of those we aim to help. We stop providing answers and start asking questions. We replace dependency with dignity. In doing so, we become not the saviors of the developing world but allies of its emerging leaders.

Charity has its place—it can mean the difference between life and death in the face of disaster. It can serve as a lifeline, a bridge over troubled waters. However, it is not the destination. If we wish to see real, lasting transformation, we must go further. We must leave the comfort of giving behind and step into the courage of equipping.

Empowerment isn't as flashy as dropping off a truckload of supplies; it's slower and sometimes messy. It requires patience and proximity. It's about handing over the hammer, not building the house for someone. It's about believing that ingenuity, resourcefulness, and leadership already exist—hidden beneath layers of poverty, trauma, and underestimation. When we empower, we acknowledge a truth that is often overlooked in philanthropic circles: people don't need pity; they need partnership.

Continual monetary donations can inadvertently foster a culture of dependence. When aid becomes routine, innovation stagnates, and local economies deteriorate. Skills that were once passed down through generations are abandoned in favor of short-term survival.

In some regions, farmers ceased planting because food aid became predictable. Markets closed as donated goods were cheaper than any locally produced items. Dreams faded since opportunities were always assumed to come from "outside."

But when communities are empowered with education, tools, capital, and decision-making power, something changes. The spark within ignites. Ownership replaces obligation. And growth becomes exponential.

Empowerment in action

- Bangladesh: In rural districts, the BRAC organization trained tens of thousands of women in small business management. One program empowered women to purchase solar lanterns and rent them out to their neighbors. The result? Clean light, additional income, and the emergence of a tech-savvy generation of entrepreneurs powered not by dollars, but by dignity.

- Peru: Quechua women in the Andes, once regarded as invisible in economic planning, received training in traditional textile weaving and connected with global markets. Within five years, entire communities became self-sustaining while preserving their cultural heritage.

- Kenya: A youth-led initiative in Nairobi's Kibera slum has established a coding bootcamp that includes donated laptops and volunteer mentors. Today, alumni are developing apps, managing businesses, and training the next generation of tech leaders—all while remaining in their neighborhood.

In each case, the common thread wasn't money; it was belief in people's ability to change their own narrative. To empower is to step into the unknown. It's more demanding than simply writing a check; it asks us to invest not only resources but also time and trust. It requires us to listen more than we speak, to ask before we act, and to let go of the hero story and walk as equals. It is not about rescuing; it is about revealing. The gold is already in the ground—we are just helping communities dig.

True empowerment is adventurous because it breaks the mold. It propels us beyond the comfort of one-time generosity into the messy, thrilling terrain of transformation. It invites us to leave the role of benefactor and become fellow travelers. When we choose empowerment over charity, we don't just help someone live another day; we help them rewrite every day that follows.

In rural Cambodia, years of war and genocide left an entire generation without access to education. NGOs rushed in with supplies and scholarships, yet a sense of ownership was still lacking.

One organization shifted its approach. Instead of simply building schools, it trained local teachers from within the community and established village education committees. Parents contributed a small monthly fee, not because the program required it, but because this contribution fostered commitment. It was successful. Dropout rates plummeted. Literacy soared. Students didn't just learn—they led. They became mentors, organizers, and advocates. Their voices became loud enough to be heard beyond the rice fields.

When I worked for the late Senator John McCain's wife, Cindy McCain, filming and writing about efforts to remove abandoned landmines in Cambodia and along Thailand's border regions, we met with children in one of these community school buildings. The dirt floors and repurposed boards indicated that the building had been constructed by the locals. However, the education they received taught them how to avoid illness from drinking contaminated water, how to stay away from areas where deadly landmines were buried, and how to read and write in English.

High above the glittering skyline of Lima, the dusty hillside of Villa El Salvador reveals makeshift homes that cling to rock and hope. Life here is hard—running water is rare, and opportunity is even rarer. But in a corner workshop filled with the hum of sewing machines, a subtle revolution is taking place. A group of women, once unemployed and overlooked, has been trained in fashion design and business management through a local empowerment initiative. Instead of simply giving out money, the program provided them with tools, mentorship, and a space to create.

They named their co-op Madres con Manos Fuertes—Mothers with Strong Hands. Now, their clothing line is sold in markets across Peru. They have employed neighbors, educated others, and even advocated to the local government for better infrastructure. They didn't wait for charity; they became the architects of their revival.

I visited one of their locations in the barrios of Lima while documenting a dental team called International Health Emissaries. Our local contacts were a couple of nuns from the convent, the Sisters of Mercy. These were no ordinary nuns; I would call them super nuns. Their superpowers were strength, love, and a belief in uplifting the impoverished. All they lacked were spandex costumes and capes.

During our tour, the pride radiating from these women was clear in their smiles. They had little, but their training as seamstresses provided them with a sense of purpose and a modest income that helped support their families. Their facility had become a hub for the community; it acted as a center for education, and this particular location had expanded to include a kitchen where younger women were taught to create delicious chocolate delicacies to sell in the local markets.

After the 2010 earthquake, the world poured billions into Haiti. Aid organizations arrived in waves, distributing food, tents, and cash.

However, years later, many communities remained fragile because, while aid had helped them survive, it didn't teach them how to thrive. I saw this firsthand.

However, in a fishing village near Jacmel, a different approach emerged. Instead of merely providing nets or money, a grassroots program trained locals in sustainable fishing, reef protection, and cooperative business models. Young individuals learned how to track their catch, market it, and manage shared profits.

Years later, the fishers are not only feeding their families, they're teaching other coastal villages to do the same. They're protecting marine life. They're leading. The biggest difference? They own the process. As a result, they will protect it with everything they have.

Here's the truth: empowerment is more challenging. It takes more time. It requires trust, cultural humility, and the willingness to step back so others can step forward. You won't always see instant results, and you won't be the hero of the story. Yet empowerment is sticky. It adheres to hearts, communities, and generations. It creates leaders, not recipients. It teaches innovation, not reliance. It invites people not just to survive but to shape their futures.

We need to stop seeing ourselves as the spark. The fire is already burning—in Cambodia's students, in Lima's mothers, in Haiti's fishers. Our role is not to ignite but to clear the path; to fan the flames.

The power of hope

When discussing empowerment, we must also address hope. Hope is a powerful and essential human emotion that provides a sense of optimism and possibility, even in difficult circumstances. It is the belief that positive outcomes are achievable and that situations can improve. Hope fuels resilience and determination, enabling individuals to endure hardships and pursue their goals with purpose. Empowerment helps individuals to discover hope within themselves.

The nature of hope is deeply rooted in human psychology and has been studied by philosophers, psychologists, and theologians throughout history. It is often seen as a driving force that propels individuals forward, enabling them to envision a better future and take action to bring about positive change. Hope can manifest in various forms, such as personal hope for individual goals or collective hope for societal progress. It can arise from multiple sources, including faith, personal experiences, supportive relationships, and inspiring role models. Hope can also be contagious, spreading from one person to another and generating a collective sense of optimism.

While hope can be a source of motivation and resilience, it is essential to strike a balance. Unrealistic or unfounded hope can lead to disappointment and disillusionment. Therefore, hope should be grounded in reality, acknowledging both the challenges and the potential for positive outcomes. The nature of hope is deeply ingrained in human experience; it provides inspiration, resilience, and a belief in the possibility of a better future. By cultivating hope within ourselves and others, we can navigate hardships and work towards realizing our desires while defining our true needs.

Curt Richter was an American physiologist and psychobiologist known for his research on stress and behavioral responses. One of his notable experiments involved studying the behavior of rats subjected to stressful conditions, such as being placed in water from which they could not escape. This experiment, known as the "swim-till-exhaustion" test, aimed at understanding the impact of stress on animals and their ability to cope with it. Richter's work contributed to our understanding of stress responses and adaptive behavior.

While listening to a podcast by Mike Rowe, I was awestruck by something his guest Jedidiah Thurner revealed about the experiments conducted by Curt Richter. While experimenting on drowning rats is cruel, the results are hard to believe. Each rat died after fifteen minutes; this was the natural time limit that the rats could tread water before losing strength and drowning. However, here is the fantastic part: a rat that was pulled out of the water, toweled off, and given only five minutes to rest before being put back into the water lasted an incredible sixty hours the second time, four hundred thirty-six times longer. The only explanation the scientist could come up with is hope. The rat knew what it felt like to be rescued; it understood that eventually, a hand would pull it out of the water and recognized what being saved felt like, which gave it hope. What can we learn about ourselves when we think of hope? Is it the same thing as faith?

Faja, Bolivia, Haiti, and Mexico City

Not long after returning from our trip to Brazil with Operation Smile, I noticed that John was changing a bit. He wasn't losing his love for humanity, but I felt he was losing interest in what we were doing. He was also pursuing a new career as a professional SCUBA instructor, with opportunities to work and live at a dive resort on the small island of Roatan, a tropical paradise a few miles off the coast of Honduras. It was a positive direction for John. He listened to our advice: step through the doors into the unknown and see what you encounter on the other side. For him, that meant living and working in paradise, both above and below the crystal blue waters of the Caribbean.

I felt envious, but I still had a job, and my filming partner was no longer with me. I knew that I couldn't handle all of the marketing work alone, nor did I want to do so. International travel is so much more enjoyable when you have a good friend to share it with. But who could I invite into my chaotic world?

The choice was effortless. John and I were known as "The Guys" when it came to adventure, stories, a bit of danger, and embracing a humanitarian way of life. Since we both had been working on the *Fear Factor Live* show at Universal Studios Orlando, we were surrounded by young, impressionable team members who often asked to tag along to exotic locations with us, even offering to help carry our gear.

Anthony Hunter was one of them. He was the only person that I felt would enhance the experience because of his video and editing skills. Also, like a dry sponge thrown into a pail of water, he would absorb everything and truly benefit from the experience, both emotionally and spiritually. Anthony, whom I will now refer to as Faja, obtained this nickname from one of the very talented comedic character actors at Universal. It references the third *Austin Powers* movie in which Gold Member speaks about Austin's father in what Dr. Evil calls a freaky-deeky Dutch accent. This random bit of renaming somehow stuck, and our beloved Anthony became known as Faja from that point on. The name stuck so well that even years later, some people had no idea who Anthony Hunter was, but they knew Faja.

Faja was the embodiment of a child at heart. Born to mixed-race parents and raised by his white mother, he was taught to be color-blind and, at that time, was a practicing Buddhist. His education had focused on TV and film production, but he excelled in camera work, particularly in editing and video graphics. He was a perfect fit for what I needed though he had never even been outside the United States. So, when Operation Smile contacted me about covering a mission to Bolivia, I relished the opportunity to invite Faja along to assist me, show him the world that John and I created, and take him into the unknown. Naturally, at the mere mention of accompanying me to Bolivia, Faja jumped at the chance, much like a ten-year-old would jump at an invitation to go to Disney World for the first time. "Adorable" is the closest word I can use to describe his actions and expressions when I brought up the idea one day while we were both working at *Fear Factor Live*.

So, it was arranged. Faja and I would fly from Orlando to São Paulo, Brazil, have a short layover, and then make our way down to Bolivia, where we would meet the rest of the volunteer team.

After landing in Bolivia, we had enough time to settle in before I introduced Faja to his first Operation Smile mission briefing. He was elated; this was the first time he had ever set foot outside of the country, and here he was in Bolivia. Historically, this nation hasn't had the soundest reputation. If you recall the Liberation Army of Bolivia and a particular guerrilla leader named Che Guevara, you'll catch my drift. We were, of course, relatively safe, but let's just say this was not your typical vacation in Italy.

When we landed in São Paulo to change flights, Faja giggled as our wheels touched down. His smile was grander than that of the Cheshire Cat from *Alice in Wonderland*. I couldn't look away from him. It filled me with joy to see another adult man understand the world as a child would, without fear, without inhibitions, and bursting with excitement for every first-time experience. I knew how it felt. I had once been in his place. I was reliving that experience through him.

On my first trip to Cambodia to tour the landmine zones with the ladies of Freedom Fields USA, I felt a similar sensation, but this time I saw everything through a child's eyes. I vividly remembered walking out of a luncheon meeting at a restaurant in Siem Reap that foreign correspondents had frequented while covering the Vietnam War. I was covering an NGO that removed remnants of war, and that connection made me feel as if I had been transported back in time. Everything around me was new: the sounds, the smells, the stories, and the feel of a stone wall built by ancient Khmer artisans. As I walked, I passed a small tree with a piece of twine tethered to it. I guessed the twine's purpose was to pull the tree away from the adjacent walkway, but it also hosted a colony of enormous ants, a kind I had never seen before. They marched in cadence toward the tree, and I paused to observe them. I must have remained in my catatonic state longer than I realized because when I finally snapped out of it, I turned to see a couple of the women watching me, much like I had been watching the ants. Melissa placed her hand on my shoulder, smiled a mother's tender smile, and said, "I love watching you see everything for the first time." She noted that I was experiencing everything through the eyes of a child, which reminded her of her first trip to Cambodia. Melissa saw in me what I saw in Faja. What a wonderful gift that is.

Faja's world of firsts continued throughout the entire mission to Bolivia, and it certainly helped me view everything in a new light.

This was not only his first trip out of the country but also his first trip with me on an Operation Smile mission. When we landed at Viru Viru International Airport in Santa Cruz, Faja began to recognize the pattern. Each time the Op-Smile teams arrive at their host destination, that airport is inundated with medical personnel, including doctors, nurses, and other volunteers. Team members, even those new to missions, are easily identified by several telltales: backpacks displaying patches and pins from previous international mission locations, Operation Smile T-shirts, and hats branded with the iconic smile logo.

Bright fluorescent orange stickers, about the size of a slice of bread, are mailed to all volunteers weeks before the mission. The stickers are to be placed on all luggage and personal items to serve as lost luggage tags, allowing any lost luggage to be sent directly to Op-Smile HQ. They also help volunteers locate each other in airports and during transportation between hotels and the mission's medical facility. By the time the entire team makes it down to retrieve their checked luggage, there are busloads of international volunteers rekindling friendships from earlier missions and many new introductions in various accents and languages.

I found the familiar face of a nurse I had worked with before and was met with a squeal and a friendly hug. I introduced Faja, found our bags, and we made our way out to the bus that would take us to our hotel, which this time was a very nice resort.

Faja and I were paired with Mark (the lead photographer and a good friend of mine) and another volunteer in a lovely four-room condo with walking access to the resort's expansive pool area. This was a significant improvement from other locations in which I had been housed during Op-Smile missions. That first night featured a traditional get-to-know-everyone dinner, followed by drinks at the pool and engaging conversation.

The next morning arrived early, bringing the task of transforming a local hospital into a surgical center focused on children's facial surgeries.

Operation Smile

For those not familiar with the organization, Operation Smile is a global nonprofit specializing in safe, effective cleft surgeries.

What is a cleft lip?

A cleft lip is a birth defect in which a baby's upper lip does not form completely during pregnancy. Instead of a continuous line, there is a gap or split in the upper lip. The opening may be a small notch in the lip or a larger gap that extends into the nose.

Clefts can happen on one side (unilateral) or both sides (bilateral) of the lip. Sometimes, cleft lips occur alongside cleft palates, where the roof of the mouth also has an opening.

Babies with cleft lips, particularly those with cleft palates, often struggle to feed. As a result, these children may fail to gain weight or suffer from malnutrition. Without proper feeding support or surgery, many infants in low-resource settings could die young simply because they cannot eat properly.

Children with unrepaired clefts can suffer from frequent infections, particularly ear infections, which may lead to hearing loss. Furthermore, speech can be significantly affected, resulting in lifelong communication challenges. In many developing countries, children born with visible facial differences often face severe stigma, bullying, and social isolation.

They may be denied education, hidden away by their families, or rejected by their communities.

In some cultures, cleft lips are misunderstood as curses, leading to discrimination or abandonment. This is particularly prevalent in regions where religions include numerous mythological effigies, such as Hinduism and various African folklore religions. During a mission in Guwahati, India, I obtained permission to interview one of the local doctors leading the new cleft palate center, in partnership with Operation Smile.

During the interview, he recounted story after story of young men and women literally locked away from society in their rooms or, worse, even in closets. Their families feared the shame and ridicule that would befall them from others, believing the child was cursed or even possessed by demons.

He spoke of a very auspicious event called the head-shaving ceremony, where young boys of a certain age have their heads shaved, recite ancient texts, and enjoy weeks of activities welcoming them to manhood.

Boys with facial deformities were not allowed to participate, limiting their opportunities for employment, marriage, or respect in society.

Without surgery, children often struggle to find work as adults. Families caring for a child with an untreated cleft frequently sink further into poverty, facing both health and social costs.

One surgery, often lasting less than an hour, can transform a child's entire future. After surgery, a child can feed normally, speak more clearly, attend school, and fully engage in society. The long-term benefits are substantial compared to the relatively low cost of surgery. This is why organizations like Operation Smile can have such an outsized impact.

As one surgeon told me, *"We take children who are stared at daily and we make them invisible."*

When they go into a developing country, Operation Smile does not permanently take over a medical facility; rather, they partner with local hospitals to temporarily transform parts of the hospital into surgical centers capable of meeting their standards for cleft surgeries.

The prep teams first conduct site visits. They assess a hospital's infrastructure—such as operating rooms, sterilization equipment, patient wards, power supply, water systems, and staffing—to determine if it can safely support high-volume surgeries. They identify gaps and safety risks based on international surgical and anesthesia standards.

If the hospital meets basic requirements or can be upgraded quickly, Operation Smile provides equipment, supplies, and volunteer staff. This may include mobile sterilization units, surgical instruments, anesthesia machines, monitoring equipment, and post-operative recovery supplies. Sometimes, they even make basic physical improvements such as fixing electrical wiring, ensuring a clean water supply, or temporarily creating additional operating room space—usually by repurposing recovery rooms.

They also supplement local hospital staff with volunteer surgeons, anesthesiologists, nurses, pediatricians, and medical records teams from around the globe. Importantly, Operation Smile collaborates with local medical professionals, offering training and mentorship as part of its mission.

For approximately one to two weeks, the hospital serves as a dedicated cleft surgical center, operating at high efficiency. Hundreds of children can be screened and treated during a single mission, depending on the team size and regional needs.

Before leaving, Operation Smile ensures that post-operative care plans are in place. They may train local nurses and doctors to monitor patients or establish local partnerships for follow-up care. If needed, they leave behind donated equipment and provide longer-term training and support so that the hospital can continue cleft care independently in the future.

In some countries, including Vietnam, Morocco, India, and the Philippines, Operation Smile ultimately helps establish permanent cleft care centers operated by local professionals trained during earlier missions.

Their model focuses on empowerment and partnership, assisting in the temporary reform or upgrade of facilities to ensure safe surgeries while also building local capacity for sustainable, ongoing care.

Once again, we encounter the powerful concept of empowerment. This is why I deeply admire Operation Smile NGO. Their mission transcends the ordinary; they journey into remote townships and villages, not just to offer life-changing surgeries for free but to weave hope and transformation into the very fabric of the community. With each visit, they don't merely leave behind physical healing; they elevate each location, imparting not only advanced surgical techniques to local healers but also bestowing the blessed gifts of knowledge, vital equipment, and connections to a sprawling global tapestry of compassionate doctors, skilled surgeons, and humanitarian warriors. Their presence sparks a radiant energy, igniting a spirit of unity and purpose that resonates long after they depart, and leaving a legacy of empowerment that echoes in the hearts of those they touch.

From time to time, we were asked to leave the safety of our well-secured surgical centers and venture into the local villages to find children from previous missions and provide updates on their recovery and how their lives have changed with the stigma literally removed from their faces.

Mark, who most likely took the original photos of the children before surgery, would retake the photos to create a side-by-side comparison, a before-and-after piece for the marketing team. I would video this process and gather useful information from the families to write blog pieces to accompany Mark's photos.

Op-Smile had great success with these dual photo pieces, these visual stories of children before and after surgery, and how their lives had improved exponentially. They often led families with doubts to take a chance and bring their children forward.

With Faja in tow, Mark and I found a local representative—this time a teenage boy—to drive us deep into the Bolivian countryside in search of a young boy whom Mark remembered from a couple of years earlier. Faja was having the time of his life; the sights, smells, and sounds of Bolivia were all new to him, and he was devouring them like a starving man would devour food.

After a two-hour car ride, we reached the area of the young boy's village. We parked alongside a row of houses, all hidden behind metal privacy fences.

"Well, what do you think, Mark? Same as usual?" I said as I rubbed his shoulders from the back seat.

"Sounds like a solid plan," he said, lighting a cigarette. Mark smoked like most people breathed—unfiltered Camels, I believe. But don't quote me on the brand.

"What's the usual?" Faja asked, eager to get out of the car and explore the Bolivian landscape.

"The usual," Mark replied, "is that we start knocking on doors."

Most of the children helped by Operation Smile become pseudo-celebrities in their villages and even in the surrounding areas. In places where outsiders are typically not welcome, showing any Op-Smile credentials nearly makes you family. People in these villages don't care what your position is within the organization; all they know is that you, in one way or another, helped one of the local children. That is enough to instill trust, even though we were strangers to their town.

"Where do we start?" Faja asked

"We start with the families and children playing in the streets, and then we start knocking on doors," Mark said between puffs on his cigarette.

We played detective for the next hour until we finally got a lead. Our local guide, the only one of us who spoke Spanish in the proper dialect, came running across a small park. He had found the young boy's mother, but there seemed to be an unpredictable hitch.

I heard Mark ask our teenage guide, "What do you mean, the six-year-old boy we are looking for is in prison?"

Time for an explanation. The prison system in Bolivia has a couple of different tiers. There are regular maximum-security prisons for society's plague, and there are what we in the US once knew as debtors' prisons.

While I am no expert on the Bolivian justice system, I can explain it from our adventurous perspective. Some prisons in Bolivia allow family members, including wives and children, to not only visit the convicted but also live with them in the prison facility. In our case, it was Father's Day, and against the mother's wishes, her son was in prison visiting his father for an unknown amount of time. In these prisons, the men were allowed to leave for work each day as long as they returned in the evening. They had to pay for their accommodation and food but could easily bribe the guards to allow things like having family members live with them for a short time.

We asked the mother if she was okay with her child staying at the local prison with her husband. Her eyes began to well up with tears as she explained that this was not her decision. It was the father's, but she would like to have her son back.

We had our young driver/interpreter obtain the woman's phone number and any information she had regarding the name and location of the facility where her son was located. Upon returning to the hospital the Op-Smile teams were using, we devised a plan.

I can honestly go on record as saying that this was Operation Smile's first and likely only prison break.

The next day, we sent a van to pick up the mother in her village and bring her to the hospital where we were working. Fortunately, the prison housing the father and the son was only a few miles away from our location. We had called the jail, informing the staff that the young boy was due for a checkup by an international team of doctors from Operation Smile, who were in town for only a short time. We told them that a transport van would come by, pick up the young boy, and deliver him back after the checkup was complete. We may have fibbed a bit.

We dropped the boy's mother off a couple of blocks away. The medical team in the van had no problem gaining access to the prison, and the small boy, now almost a local celebrity, was paraded out to our medical team and released. Two blocks away, we picked up the mother. After taking a few photos of the happy reunion, we took the two back to their village. Operation Smile had pulled off a prison break.

The remainder of the mission unfolded with the thrilling unpredictability characteristic of such endeavors: countless children received brilliant new smiles, unlocking doors to brighter futures. New friendships blossomed in the heat of the moment, lives were transformed against all odds, and Faja stepped boldly into his inaugural international humanitarian expedition. Just as I had foreseen, he was now irresistibly captivated, his spirit ignited with a fervent desire for more adventure.

Knowing his answer would be a resounding "Fuck yes, I'm in," I asked him to join me for the next Operation Smile mission. It would take us to Mexico City to accompany and document a very affluent Hollywood name who had been a staunch supporter of the NGO for many years.

Brooke Burke is not only beautiful on the outside; she also has the heart of an angel. She has been an outspoken advocate for Operation Smile for more years than I have been working with them. Brooke uses her Hollywood influence to help draw attention to the incredible work the organization has been doing globally, and she often appears at the annual Operation Smile gala in Los Angeles as a brand ambassador.

On this trip, Faja, Mark, and I would accompany Brooke, her then-husband David Charvet, who is mostly known for a brief appearance on *Baywatch*, and two of her daughters, Neriah and Rain. Brooke was, and still is, one of my favorite people. Her internal beauty is not overshadowed by her external appearance, and her maternal, caring side is so obvious—not only with her own children but nearly every other child she meets. When she picked up a crying child during the screening days, it would look into her eyes and simply become content. David, on the other hand, seemed to be focused only on gaining screen time to promote his good deeds. He would complain when the daughters interrupted him while he was trying to make an emotional pitch for the NGO, complete with crocodile tears.

It didn't surprise me to hear that he and Brooke had separated a couple of years after the Mexico mission trip, filing for irreconcilable differences. I often think I missed my chance; had she been on a solo mission, who knows what cards the universe might have dealt me? There was one time when the group of us had an adult beverage night at Brooke and David's suite. Tequila was flowing, and Charvet was critiquing Neriah as she sang *Titanium* by David Guetta. I was sitting on the back of the couch laughing at Faja because he just kept looking at me, thanking me for bringing him on the adventure. The drinks were giving us all a touch of the spirit.

Brooke, who was sitting in front of me, reached up, grabbed my shirt, and pulled me down closer to speak to me. For the life of me, I still can't remember exactly what she said; it might have been a simple thank you for documenting this mission. The one thing that is and will always be locked away in my memories is the forward way she pulled me close and the sensation of her warm breath whispering in my ear. I'm glad that Faja was there as my witness. Everything Brooke did, she did with a natural seduction, including softly talking in my ear. My heart skipped a beat, and I melted into the couch. Some things we never forget.

Since he now had two Operation Smile missions under his belt, I decided to throw Faja to the lions and take him to Haiti with me to document a human and sex trafficking awareness organization that had partnered with my friends at the Haitian Christian Mission.

Back to my first Haiti experience

On my first trip to Haiti, while following my lovely nurse friend, I was introduced to Wendy Zehner, Haiti's very own Mother Teresa.

Even with its constant dangers and extreme poverty, something intriguing about the country captured my heart. Perhaps it was the people Wendy introduced me to—the ones trying to survive: the mothers, children, and families randomly dealt a bad hand by the universe. Or perhaps it was the land itself; Haiti felt as if it were lost in time.

Even though that trip lasted less than a week, I encountered new truths moment by moment. I felt like a child experiencing life through fresh eyes. It was grounding to realize that there are places in the world like this—forgotten by man yet created by God as a training ground for those seeking to learn about humanity.

Upon arrival, after the friendly handshakes and greetings, Wendy led us into the main building on the compound, which housed the kitchen, dorm rooms, and a multifunctional great room that served as the dining hall, meeting room, praise area on Sundays, and place for evening discussions and the nightly impromptu music sessions.

One of my favorite spots at the compound was a rooftop area where volunteers and staff could relax, have a few beers, and wind down while watching the sun set over the humid island skyline. From a good vantage point, you could see the ocean in the distance. This far from the larger cities, Haiti was still beautiful.

Haitian Christian Mission served many functions. It included a school that catered to children from primary grades to high school. Although they all learned in the same classroom at the same time, the lesson plans were tailored to the age and abilities of each child.

There was a weekly clinic held on the open-air porch and courtyard. Food for those in need was always available; Wendy would turn no one away. Workshops and gardens behind the main buildings provided both income and upkeep for the compound. Most importantly, apart from its spiritual environment, HCM functioned as a working medical facility that rivaled the fictional hospital from the 1970s TV series *M.A.S.H.* (Mobile Army Surgical Hospital).

The cases this small medical facility accepted were limited to... well, there were no limits. Women going into labor would knock on the front gate at all hours. Bodies, with wounds from vehicle accidents to brutal machete fights, were found at the front gate. Some were alive, some already dead. People with fractured arms or who had contracted infectious diseases, such as AIDS or cholera, would stumble in daily.

This made HCM an ideal training ground for young American doctors and nurses in training. Owing to the lack of regulations, medical students were permitted to perform procedures they would never be allowed to do back in the States.

Let me put that last statement into a clearer perspective. In the US, doctors in training practice procedures on cadavers or advanced medical dummies, some of which are robotic. In Haiti, students are permitted to train on living patients. If the procedure—supervised by highly qualified doctors—does not go as planned, no one is scolded, sued, or thrown in prison. The locals consider this normal; they are very happy to be treated by any white-skinned person, especially if they are American.

The medical facility was divided into two areas: the clinic side, which was located beneath the main dorm facility, housed the storage areas that contained the pharmacy, a clerical office, and a few small concrete rooms with a bed but no power.

The surgical center, complete with a small neonatal intensive care unit (NICU), was located in a secondary building a short walk from the main building. This is where the medical students were allowed to perform everything from sutures and amputations to cesarean sections and... well, anything else that needed to be done. To a US citizen, it's quite scary what you can get away with in a country like Haiti. But the reality is that the medical students who traveled to Haiti to practice came home with more real-world experience than their peers who had practiced on nonliving patients.

One evening, while hanging out with the students and drinking beer in the main gathering hall, one of the local women working at HCM ran into the room to inform us that a middle-aged woman had been dropped off at the front gates. She was unconscious and barely breathing. There was no time to take her to the surgical center, so we laid her out on the concrete floor in the best-lit area we could find. The reality of the situation was that the chief medical trainer, after a brief exam, had concluded that the woman was not going to live, but he didn't share this information with his students—I found this out later, during an interview. He let them work on her as if they had a chance of saving her life. It drove them into a frenzy of humanity and love. They worked on her believing they could save her. It was an amazing training scenario to witness.

The woman eventually coded, which meant that her heart stopped. The training doctor asked for the paddles—a slang term for the cardiac defibrillation unit—so the students could practice cardioverting a human heart. One of the nurses informed us that the unit was at the surgical center on the opposite side of the compound. I volunteered to run and get it.

With a beer in my right hand and the defibrillator in my left, I sprinted back to the clinic area and handed off the unit to a handful of anxious medical students who took no time at all to charge the paddles, yell "clear", and begin the attempt to shock the woman back to life. The truth was that her heart had already stopped beating.

In movies, especially low-budget ones, you always see hospital scenes in which a heart monitor flatlines, emitting the well-known, solid beeping sound. Then people rush in and start shocking the shit out of the person, causing the body to convulse violently and rise off the bed. Although it looks good on film, that's not how cardioversion works. You can't shock a flatline. The process of cardioversion is actually to convert the heart rhythm, meaning that there must be a heart rhythm to convert.

This woman was well past that point, but the real, hands-on experience the students received was invaluable to their training—and something they could never have done back in the States.

One day, we visited a shady warehouse where Wendy haggled over the price of fifty-pound bags of rice, which the staff portioned into individual servings for delivery to a small village on the far side of Lake Azuei which was accessible only by a homemade, very leaky rowboat.

Lake Azuéi, also known as Étang Saumâtre, is Haiti's largest lake and a significant natural landmark. Located approximately 18 miles (29 kilometers) east of Port-au-Prince, it straddles the border with the Dominican Republic in the Plaine du Cul-de-Sac region.

Covering an area of about 170 square kilometers, Lake Azuéi is a brackish lake, meaning its water has a higher salinity than freshwater but lower than seawater. The lake's intense blue waters are surrounded by diverse ecosystems, including dry shrublands and wetlands. It supports over 100 species of waterfowl, such as American flamingos, and is one of the few habitats in Haiti for the American crocodile. Had I known about the crocodile infestation, I might have chosen to opt out of this trip,

Another day, the front wheel of our van flew off and shot into a streetside shanty town as we were on our way back from a trip to buy frozen chicken and root vegetables from a large market for dinner that evening. The market was stifling, smelled like rotting garbage, and was located along the rear wall of Haiti's maximum-security prison.

Haiti presented daily adventures, whether we wanted them or not. One day, we loaded the vans—all with their wheels intact—with medical supplies and traveled half a day into the desert mountains to a church, where we set up a mobile clinic to assist those who couldn't make it down to the HCM compound.

That day, Edwens took Eva and me to a beautiful jungle resort for lunch and drinks. The resort was near the president's house and he wanted to show us the two-mile driveway that led up to the current president's house. It had been paved with custom, hand-laid paver stones purchased with donations from the U.S. for the earthquake relief fund. It was a potent demonstration of the Haitian government's corruption.

The evening after our resort visit, we were thrust back into the reality of life in Haiti. As usual, it began with someone pounding on the metal gate, yelling for assistance from the dark street on the other side. By the time we got downstairs, the guard had partially opened the gate, allowing a couple of locals to drop off a very pregnant woman.

Eva and Wendy ran over to the woman, who was alone and leaning against the steps of the small guard shack. Wendy hollered to one of the men on the staff to bring one of the vans over because we needed to transport the woman to a nearby birthing hospital. Eva jumped into action and started an assessment while Wendy went in to grab a blanket and a couple of the medical students to help us out.

A short time later, we had the pregnant woman strapped to a makeshift backboard. Due to the width of the van, we had to slide the board over the top of the seats, spanning three rows like a bridge. Her feet were aimed back with her head facing forward toward Eva, who was in the front seat, sitting backward and communicating with the young woman. The rest of us were seated in each row, holding the backboard securely as our driver flew, and I mean flew, through the streets to the hospital.

Upon arriving at the location, we pulled up in front of a dimly lit building and were met by a guard who assisted us in getting the woman safely from our van. What I witnessed next left an image painted in my mind that will never leave.

Entering the building was the first challenge. As with many buildings in Haiti, there was no elevator, at least not a working one. This meant that the four of us had to carry the backboard up two flights of stairs to reach the entrance door on the second floor. I don't know what I was expecting to see, but what I actually saw, and smelled is hard to put into words. On the other side of the door was a long hallway; its filthy concrete floor was stained with bodily fluids—blood and amniotic fluid. Some areas were wet, other spots were sticky. A couple of failing fluorescent lights flickered, lighting the horror movie scene.

Lining the hallway, on the unsterile concrete floor were pregnant women, lots of pregnant women who all appeared to be moments away from giving birth. The women were sitting upright, leaning back against a cinderblock wall, with large, stained plastic bowls of varying colors positioned between their spread legs. The bowls were there to catch the fluid when their water broke, or whatever else came out, including the occasional baby. It was a scene from hell, something you'd see painted on the walls of a Roman cathedral representing Dante's *Inferno.*

Our patient received extra attention, possibly due to the way we barged in and because the infant was already crowning. The hospital staff took the young lady into a room filled with, you guessed it, more pregnant women. This time, they were all on birthing tables, feet in stirrups, and in different stages of delivery. I refused to allow myself to focus on anything—some things you just can't unsee. I didn't need another one of those images stuck in my memories.

The drive back was somewhat less chaotic and included a stop for cold beer and a bottle of tequila. We were all exhausted from the event. After taking cold showers, we all went up to the roof to relax, enjoy some adult beverages, and de-stress.

I slept well that night. Haiti, of all places, was growing on me. The danger and excitement only made the mission more enjoyable—from the barren desert mountains, the lake crossings, the medical stuff I was thrown into, the people, and of course, the amazing HCM compound. I witnessed births and deaths, and beautiful sunrises and sunsets, and I truly connected with the people and the land itself. Something energetic flowed through me, pushing me to want to do and help more. It's as if Haiti were alive and communicating directly with my soul.

Humans, Compassion, and Earthly Energy

Humans are connected to the energy of the Earth in several profound ways: biologically, electrically, and spiritually. The Earth has a natural electromagnetic field, and humans possess one as well. Practices like grounding or earthing (walking barefoot on natural ground) are believed to enable the body to absorb the Earth's electrons, potentially reducing inflammation, improving sleep, and balancing the nervous system.

Our bodies are synchronized with the Earth's cycles, particularly the light-dark cycle of the sun, known as circadian rhythms. This connection regulates sleep, hormone production, and mental well-being.

Some researchers suggest that the human brain and heart resonate with the Earth's Schumann Resonance (about 7.83 Hz), a frequency generated by lightning and atmospheric activity. This resonance may influence brainwave states, intuition, and overall well-being.

We are literally made of Earth—our bodies are composed of water, minerals, and elements that originate from the planet. We embody elemental interdependence; we breathe its air, eat its food, and are sustained by its ecosystems. Many indigenous and spiritual traditions teach that the Earth is a living entity and that humans are spiritually connected to it. This perspective encourages harmony, respect, and stewardship.

Yes, the energy of the Earth can lead humans back to humanity—if we define humanity as our innate capacity for empathy, connection, and harmony with life. Reconnecting physically with the Earth through nature, stillness, or touch pulls us out of distraction and into the present moment. In that state, people tend to become more reflective, compassionate, and aware of others.

Nature mirrors balance

The cycles of the Earth—birth, decay, renewal—remind us of our shared vulnerabilities and interdependence. This can dissolve ego and awaken a sense of kinship, both with one another and with all life. Energetic resonance softens isolation. When people spend time attuned to the Earth's energy (via grounding, forest immersion, or meditation), it often lowers anxiety and boosts emotional sensitivity. That emotional clarity makes room for empathy and reconnection.

Indigenous and ancient cultures often see the Earth not merely as a source of sustenance, but as a teacher.

By listening to the rhythms of nature, people are reminded of humility, patience, and generosity—core aspects of our shared humanity. So yes—by tuning into the Earth's energy, they often remember what it means to be human in a deeper, more connected sense.

Nature mirrors balance through its rhythms, systems, and silent intelligence—revealing how all life exists in dynamic harmony, even amid chaos. Nature continuously moves through cycles—day and night, seasons, birth and decay. These cycles demonstrate that death is not an end, but a transition. In this, we learn that letting go is a vital part of renewal.

Every organism plays a role. Predators help keep populations in check; plants purify the air; fungi decompose and recycle nutrients. Nothing exists in isolation. Balance arises from mutual support and diversity. Nature responds to disturbance not by collapsing but by adapting. Forests regrow after fires. Rivers carve new paths following floods.

Balance isn't rigid; it's a flexible alignment with changing conditions. From the spiral of a nautilus shell to the branching of trees and blood vessels, natural forms reflect patterns of proportional growth. These fractals and golden ratios symbolize balance in form and function.

Nature moves in rhythms—like the tide, the heartbeat of the ocean. Yet it also offers stillness: a mountain, a quiet forest. It teaches that balance encompasses both action and rest, movement and pause.

In all of this, nature doesn't strive—it simply exists. That quiet equilibrium invites us to discover balance within ourselves: to give and receive, to act and reflect, to grow and release.

Nature is the original teacher of balance—not through instruction, but through quiet demonstration. In its cycles of birth, growth, decay, and renewal, we see that life is not linear but rhythmic, always moving between opposites: light and dark, stillness and motion, giving and receiving. Ecosystems thrive not by dominance but through interdependence—each organism plays a role, each part supports the whole. Forests recover after fire, rivers change course after floods, and life continues, not by resisting change but by adapting to it. Even the patterns etched into leaves, shells, and galaxies reflect a deeper symmetry that governs both beauty and function.

In observing nature, we are reminded that balance is not perfection or control—it is a living harmony that encompasses chaos, loss, and renewal. By aligning with this natural rhythm, we find a path back to ourselves and return to a more grounded, human way of being.

When we tune into nature's rhythm, we begin to hear something quieter yet deeply familiar—our own intuition. Just as the Earth knows when to bloom and when to rest, we too carry an inner wisdom that guides us beyond logic. However, in a world filled with noise and urgency, that voice is often drowned out.

Nature invites us to slow down and listen again. In the hush of a forest or the rhythm of waves, we remember that we are not separate from the Earth's intelligence, we are part of it. This reconnection is not just calming; it's empowering. Intuition rooted in stillness gives us the courage to trust ourselves, act with clarity, and respond with heart instead of habit. By regaining our place within nature's balance, we reclaim a deeper, more authentic power—the power to live in alignment with who we truly are: loving, caring, compassionate beings.

About a year after my first trip to Haiti with Eva, Wendy called to ask if I could please come back down and document a couple of organizations that HCM had recently teamed up with. One group had donated new incubators for their new NICU unit in the expanding surgical center. The other group, Rapha House, was an NGO that helped raise awareness about human trafficking, specifically focused on child sex trafficking. The organization already had safe houses and counselors in Cambodia and Thailand, where the sex trade runs rampant.

Haiti faced an issue with children being sexually exploited, but the situation was different and, in some ways, much worse.

Human Trafficking Haitian Style

Let's start with some information on child sex trafficking. We have all been hearing a lot of press about human trafficking and children disappearing due to the situation at the southern border of the United States. How can one put this gently? Let's say that there are a few gaps in the border and that a large number of unescorted children have been crossing through the gaps over the past four years.

Trafficking has been a global crisis for decades. The sex trade follows events like the Super Bowl, the World Cup, and even the Olympics. It's still touted as the oldest profession in the world.

However, adults choosing to pursue that path and children being forced into the industry are entirely separate topics.

Haiti is in a world of its own, with many factors leading to its current horrific situation. Extenuating circumstances have created a worse problem than when I was down there documenting Rapha House. Child sex trafficking in Haiti remains a severe and escalating crisis, exacerbated by widespread gang violence, poverty, and the collapse of essential services.

Between 2023 and 2024, the recruitment of children by armed groups in Haiti surged by 70%, with minors constituting 30% to 50% of gang members. Children as young as eight are coerced or abducted into gangs, often under threats to their families.

Boys are typically used as informants or combatants, while girls are subjected to domestic servitude and sexual exploitation. The situation is dire in Port-au-Prince, where gangs control approximately 85% of the city. Over a million people, half of whom are children, are displaced due to ongoing violence. Many live in makeshift shelters, rendering them vulnerable to recruitment and abuse.

Sexual violence against children has escalated dramatically, with reports of armed groups inflicting "unimaginable horrors" on minors. Girls are often abducted, beaten, drugged, and raped, sometimes over extended periods. UNICEF has described children's bodies as "battlegrounds" in the ongoing conflict.

The border between Haiti and the Dominican Republic represents another area of concern. Children crossing without documentation face an increased risk of trafficking and exploitation.

UNICEF and the Haitian government are intensifying efforts to prevent child recruitment and strengthen reintegration programs. Initiatives include training security forces and civil society organizations on child protection measures.

However, funding continues to be a significant challenge. UNICEF's 2024 emergency funding appeal for Haiti was 72% underfunded, hindering the provision of essential services to vulnerable children. The international community continues to monitor the situation, with various organizations emphasizing the urgent need for comprehensive interventions to protect Haiti's children from trafficking and exploitation.

Extreme poverty and a corrupt government contribute to Haiti's challenges. Many organizations, both governmental and non-governmental, have good intentions in their efforts, but their messages often go unheard by a significant portion of the local population, particularly among men.

Along with sex education classes aimed at curbing the rampant spread of diseases like Hepatitis and AIDS, thousands of condoms were shipped and handed out like candy on Halloween night. Ill-fitting, non-lubricated condom wrappers litter the streets. Men won't use them because they take all the pleasure out of intercourse; however, children find that they make fantastic balloons. I am not exaggerating or trying to make light of the situation. I have seen many children walking along the roadside with inflated condoms tied to strings and sticks.

It pains me to write this, but the hardcore truth is that if a man is actively in the process of raping a woman or, even worse, an innocent child, the last thing on his mind is using a condom.

Poverty also drives women and mothers to engage in activities that, in the States, could lead to imprisonment or worse. Sex is often free. As I observed in the birthing center, many children grow up never knowing their fathers. Single women of all ages have multiple children by different men, some through consensual acts and some not.

If you are born a boy by chance, you can work, steal, or engage in activities that help bring food or money into your household. Alternatively, you can join a gang or take to the streets. If you are born a girl and your family lives in extreme poverty, you are simply another mouth to feed.

This leads me to write about one of the most disturbing things I have ever witnessed, mothers selling their daughters for sex. This is why Rapha House went to Haiti—to investigate this horrific act.

Mothers would often take their daughters, some as young as six or seven, to the ports and prostitute them to the sailors and dock workers for twenty-five cents a turn. Yes, you read that correctly, one US quarter, twenty-five copper pennies, is all it takes to buy the innocence of a young girl in certain locations in Haiti.

The question is, where does the blame lie? The mother doesn't believe that she is doing anything wrong; the young girl has become a commodity instead of a burden. Rather than a mouth to feed, she serves a purpose.

The blame must fall on the monsters with a pocket full of change and a hunger for children. It disgusts me even to have been told this information. Education and empowerment are the only ways to help children in areas like Haiti; however, I fear that with the current conditions in the country, the road to healing will be very long. And very bumpy.

The first call I made after getting off the phone with Wendy was to Faja, who jumped at the opportunity to add another stamp to his passport. I went over the plan: where we were staying, how we were getting around, what we were documenting, and, most of all, I gave him my speech on how Haiti was like nowhere else I had ever taken him.

A couple of weeks later, we were on a southbound flight out of Miami, and I was looking forward to getting back to the compound for a bit of adventure, Haitian style. Edwens had been constructing a new three-story apartment and office building at the rear of the surgical center. It was a place from which he and Wendy could run HCM and its expanding medical facility. Its construction was simple but a bit more modern than the main compound, and from the rooftop balcony, there was a fantastic view of the tropical ocean skyline.

Due to the large number of medical students and volunteers during our trip, the new office also served as a place for Faja and me to stay while we were there.

As with my first trip to Haiti with Eva, Wendy ensured that Faja received a detailed tour of the island. We took him to the refugee camps, crossed the lake in the leaky rowboats to deliver supplies to the village, and packed up the medical teams in the vans, setting up mobile clinics in Port-au-Prince and its surrounding townships. Faja was inundated with new experiences, and like me, he was loving every moment of the escapade.

But with the highs come the lows. On our last full day there, we were asked to film a short piece about the newly refurbished neonatal intensive care unit, which includes three infant incubators donated by a dedicated female doctor committed to helping reduce Haiti's infant mortality rate.

The mortality rate in Haiti was 40 deaths per 1,000, compared to 5.5 per 1,000 live births in the US. This became a day that put me in a filming position that will never leave my memories.

If began like any other day ... just as typical as a day at a medical encampment in Haiti can be. Faja and I came down for coffee, breakfast, and morning conversations before walking over to the surgical center. We had a game plan, but many of our video segments developed organically due to the unpredictable nature of global humanitarian missions.

We started filming some B-roll, which means random shots with no dialogue or interviews. Faja had brought a device with four wheels, about the size of a roller-skate, to mount his camera on; the smooth movement added production value to the shots. While he was doing his thing, I meandered through the surgical center, talking to the nurses and looking for something interesting to capture.

Wendy popped her head through the open door of the room I was in to tell me that we might have a good story to document. I followed her down the hall to a closed door on the right. I walked in with her to find a young pregnant woman lying on an examination table; I could tell by the look on the doctor's face that something wasn't right.

After conducting a manual exam and not receiving the desired response, the doctor connected the ultrasound to attempt to locate a fetal heartbeat. Time seemed to stand still. I snapped a few shots of the doctor during the procedure and then switched to my video camera to see if I could catch some good audio of the dialogue being had through a local nurse translating the English to Creole conversation.

"Your baby has no heartbeat" the doctor said to the woman. Her words hung heavy in the room as they were translated to the young woman on the table. "Your baby is dead." As she spoke, a single tear ran down her cheek. There was so much compassion in the room.

The young pregnant woman's sister, who had accompanied her, was sitting in the room with the incubators, engaging in conversation with Wendy. In the sister's arms was a newborn baby boy—a baby we assumed was hers, the sister's. After a brief conversation, Wendy requested that the doctor come to talk. I followed her. What we learned sucked the air from the room and turned us pale.

The story relayed to us was that the infant in the woman's arms was not hers but her sister's, the one on the table with the stillborn infant still inside her. As it turned out, the woman was pregnant with twins and had delivered the healthy male at her house close to a week earlier; however, the second baby, the twin sister, could not be delivered. Her family took her to a Voodoo doctor for help.

Voodoo is a legitimate religion; it is rooted in Christianity and remains a dominant religious practice in Haiti.

As reality hit, so did the alarm. The stillborn had been in the woman for close to a week. She had been walking around with a full-term dead infant inside of her. Death was imminent; the young woman's body regarded the fetus as an infection. If the doctors couldn't remove it, the woman would die within days.

We all hurried back to the examination room, where the doctor informed the woman that we were going to transfer her to the operating theater in an effort to remove the fetus. Moments later, as the door closed with me inside, I wasn't sure if I was prepared for what I was about to witness.

As I previously realized while filming children's facial surgeries with Operation Smile, looking at a monitor or through the video camera's lens shields you from what is actually happening in front of you. I still have a hard time watching surgeries, but I have no issues filming them.

After a couple of attempts to guide the fetus out through the way nature intended, the doctor called for an epidural. If you're not sure what an epidermal is, I can tell you that it's not the most pleasant thing to watch being administered.

Getting an epidural, commonly used for pain relief during labor and certain surgeries, involves a series of carefully controlled steps performed by an anesthesiologist or nurse anesthetist. The advantage of an epidural is that the patient remains awake throughout the entire surgical procedure, with the ability to communicate with the doctors and nurses in the room. It also alleviates any potential issues with being fully put under anesthesia.

Typically, in the US or any other first-world country, the procedure is pretty straightforward. The medical provider explains the procedure, risks, and benefits. You'll be asked to sign a consent form. Vital signs like blood pressure, heart rate, and oxygen levels are monitored. An IV line is usually placed to administer fluids or medications.

You will be asked to sit up or lie on your side, arching your back and remaining as still as possible to open the spaces between the vertebrae. The lower back is cleaned with an antiseptic solution to minimize the risk of infection.

A local anesthetic is injected into the skin to numb the area where the epidural needle will be inserted. You may experience a brief sting or burn. Then, a special hollow needle is carefully inserted into the epidural space (just outside the spinal cord's protective covering). Through this needle, a thin, flexible catheter is threaded into the epidural space. The needle is removed, leaving the catheter in place, which is secured to your back with tape to keep it in position.

Pain-relieving medication, typically a mix of anesthetics and/or opioids, is administered through the catheter. Relief usually begins within 10 to 20 minutes. The medication can be given as a continuous infusion or in periodic doses throughout labor or surgery.

In layman's terms, an epidural pretty much paralyzes the body from the point of insertion down through the rest of the body. There is no feeling, thus no pain.

At least, this is how it would be under ideal conditions. We, however, were in Haiti at a free medical center that was understaffed and had limited supplies.

Our young woman was placed in a seated position on the operating table. From behind her, the doctor inserted the needle into a slightly numbed area while a nurse hurried to set up an IV in the woman's arm. Everything was moving fast. All the correct steps were taken, but this was an emergency, so the medical team only had one shot to save the mother's life.

After about ten minutes had passed, and using one of the nurses to interpret, the doctor established that the woman was completely numb from the chest down. Then, she began the C-section to remove the dead fetus.

I hid behind my camera and tried to keep the operation in frame and in focus. I've had the opportunity to film some fascinating surgeries in remarkable locations around the globe. This was by far the most intense.

It had been some time since I was in a room while a surgery was going on. Along with documenting, my second mission was to not pass out. It's just something that your body does from time to time without asking you for permission. I found a good vantage point, leaned back against a wall, and took some deep breaths, inhaling through the mouth to avoid the fragrant aroma of flesh being cauterized, along with the distinct iron smell of blood.

The other thing that many people never get the chance to witness, or want to, is just how aggressive many surgeries can be; especially when performed under less than perfect conditions and when there is a rush to save a life.

Our doctor wasted no time in cutting into the young mother. A C-section is not a pretty thing to watch. To get to the womb, where the fetus is located, one must first cut through the skin and fat covering the abdomen, followed by the abdominal muscles while trying to avoid any vital organs that might present themselves.

It's not a small incision either. To remove a full-size infant, you have to cut most of the way across the belly area. In a U.S. medical facility, with a sterile environment, the latest modern medical equipment, and plenty of extra hands, the procedure I was filming might have looked a bit more… delicate, for lack of a better word. However, there was nothing delicate happening here.

Once the doctor had cut deep enough, she began to insert her gloved hands into the opening, rooting around in an attempt to find the baby. The first thing I remember seeing was her hand emerge with a small pale foot, and then the second one. From that point, she forcefully pulled the dead fetus from the womb, along with the amniotic sac and everything else that would typically be expelled as afterbirth during a normal, healthy vaginal childbirth.

I remember being shocked by the size of the body as it was handed off to Wendy to wrap it in a blanket and keep it out of the young mother's view. The whole situation was insane. One minute, a young mother is seeking help with her pregnancy, and the next, she is on a table being ripped open.

But if you ever wanted to see a room filled with overflowing compassion, this was it. Strangers saving strangers' lives without a hint of monetary concern or desire for status. There would be no posting on social media; no look at what I did. No sing my praises to the masses. The doctor and her non-profit organization called Labor of Love stayed true to its name right in front of my lens.

That night, after such a traumatic day for all of us, we took some time to debrief and unload on each other over a few beers. Faja could see that what I had filmed was affecting me a bit. It was, in many ways. The graphic nature of what I had filmed was still fresh in my mind's eye, but it was overshadowed by the love and admiration I felt for this small band of volunteer doctors, nurses, medical students, and even some young high school students volunteering on their school break.

This is why I will always sing the praises of my friends at HCM and why Haiti will always hold a place in my heart. Just as strangers help strangers during natural disasters, locations across the globe, like Haiti, provide the world with rare opportunities to develop personal skills such as empathy and compassion for humanity, enabling us to rise from the rubble of an imperfect world.

When Hearts Speak: Compassion as Our Oldest Instinct

I can recall the first time I felt compassion seep into my heart. It punched me directly in the soul.

I couldn't have been much more than six years old. It was a cold, rainy Christmas Eve night. My mother and I were coming home from a last-minute gift drop-off, and I was anxious to get home and in bed so that Santa would visit my house, inundating my Christmas morning with toys beyond my wildest imagination.

Then it happened. God showed me who I was to become. I was bundled up in my jacket on a rare frigid Florida evening, and it happened right there, in the passenger seat of our car. It was not my choice.

The traffic light we were approaching turned yellow and then red. Mom slowed our blue Ford station wagon to a stop at the intersection; our windows were lightly fogged due to the temperature difference outside and inside. I saw him as mom used her gloved hand to wipe away the haze on the windshield's interior and her driver's side window.

A homeless man was sleeping in a covered bus stop. He was sheltered from the rain but not from the cold. My six-year-old heart broke as empathy rushed through my body; it was a new sensation. I always felt sympathy for stray animals, but not for stray people. Not until then.

I looked at my mother with tears in my eyes and said, "It's not fair." My developing mind couldn't understand why this man was without a place to go on Christmas Eve. Where was his family? Why was he all alone on this cold, rainy night—the day before Christmas?

I remember asking my mother if we could take him home with us because he deserved to be in a warm house for the holidays, surrounded by people instead of being alone on a bench in the elements.

She declined my request to take the man home, which was probably a good parental decision. However, she sensed the explosion of feelings emanating from my little soul.

I fell asleep that night, torn between the excitement of the next morning, anticipating the arrival of the white-bearded guy in the big red suit, and the sadness I felt for the man at the bus stop. From that day on, my superpower was empathy, whether I wanted it or not.

Empathy is the thrilling spark that ignites compassion in our hearts, driving us on a daring quest to connect with others. If you unravel the word "compassion," you'll discover the fiery essence of "passion" nestled within. Those who embody empathy and extend compassion are fueled by an adventurous spirit, an intrinsic passion that compels them to explore the depths of human connection and generosity.

The prefix "com-" in "compassion" is derived from Latin and means "with" or "together." In compassion, it combines with "passion" (from the Latin passio, meaning "suffering" or "enduring") to create the idea of "suffering with" someone—feeling and sharing another's pain or hardship.

Chase your dreams with reckless abandon! Seek out exhilarating human connections; life is an adventure meant to be fully embraced, and sharing your spirit freely can energize your mind, invigorate your body, and even transform your soul for the adventures that lie beyond!

There is a thread running through every living creature, woven deeper than sight and sound. It is the silent language of feeling—the ability to sense joy, fear, hurt, or hope in another being without a single word spoken. This is compassion—a force as real and vital as any of our five senses.

Scientists might say it is empathy, rooted in mirror neurons firing quietly in our brains. Poets might call it a soul's recognition of itself in another. But anyone who has ever sat beside a grieving friend or knelt before a wounded animal knows the truth:

Compassion is a feeling. It is a way of understanding.

Even in the first moments of life, a newborn baby cries upon hearing another infant's cries. They do not yet understand hunger or loneliness, but they instinctively feel the echo of another's pain and respond. Compassion is not taught; it is inherited, as ancient and instinctive as the beating of our hearts.

Animals recognize this too. A mother elephant will pause for hours with the body of her lost calf, gently touching it with her trunk and refusing to leave it behind. Dogs whimper when their owners are sick or sad, curling up protectively beside them. A herd of wildebeests will slow its pace for an injured member, defying their instinct for speed and risking danger rather than leaving one behind.

There is wisdom in this—a wisdom older than reason. It tells us that we are not separate. Your pain is not only yours; it ripples outward, felt in the hearts of others. It is an invisible current flowing between beings. When we allow ourselves to tune into this sixth sense, the world changes.

A child we have never met cries out across a crowded market, and without thinking, we move toward them. A stranger's grief catches in our throats. A glimpse of suffering—even halfway across the world, in a photograph or a story—tugs at something deep within us.

This ability to feel what another feels is not a weakness. It is a strength. It has allowed humanity to survive, build communities, and dream beyond our small hungers.

It binds parents to children, neighbors to neighbors, and nations to nations. Yet compassion is more than mere survival; it makes us fully human.

It calls us to action—not out of obligation, but because something within us knows we cannot stand aside and remain whole.

In a world that is growing louder, faster, and harsher, we are often taught to shield ourselves, closing off this sixth sense for fear of being overwhelmed. But when we do, something essential withers inside us.

We lose the sharpness of our sight, the sweetness of our hearing, and the warmth of our touch—because compassion is the thread that ties all our senses together.

The great secret is this: The more we allow ourselves to feel the pain of others, the greater our capacity for joy, love, and courage.

Compassion does not empty us—it expands us. It is not a burden—it is a bridge. It connects a mother in Malawi to a surgeon in another land. It links a stranger's tear to a volunteer's outstretched hand. It binds a world fractured by fear into something closer to family.

We do not walk alone when we live with compassion as a sixth sense. We move through life with an invisible network of hearts beating alongside our own—a chorus of hope, a symphony of connection. And perhaps, if we listen closely enough, we can hear it even now—the quiet pulse of one heart reaching out to another, across distance, across difference, and across the vast, beautiful mystery of being alive.

Here's a list of actions we, as human beings, can take or practice to deepen our compassion toward others:

- Slow down and pay attention: Compassion begins with noticing. When we move too fast, we overlook the subtle signals of others' struggles—the tired eyes, the forced smiles, the silence. Practice slowing down, making eye contact, and genuinely seeing people. Compassion often starts by simply paying attention to what isn't being said.

- Listen without planning your response: Most people listen to reply, not to understand. Practice listening purely to receive another person's experience, without rushing to fix, judge, or add your own story. True listening is an act of profound respect and a doorway to compassion.

- Imagine their inner world: Everyone you meet is carrying a story you cannot see, full of fears, losses, dreams, and regrets. Practice envisioning the invisible burdens others might bear. When you encounter a rude stranger, a crying child, or an impatient coworker, ask yourself: What pain might lie behind that face?

- Choose curiosity over judgment; When someone behaves in ways you don't understand, practice asking yourself: "I wonder what brought them here?" instead of "What's wrong with them?" Curiosity softens the heart; judgment hardens it.

- Practice small acts of kindness daily: Smile, hold a door open, or send a message to someone who crosses your mind. Small, intentional acts of kindness create pathways in your brain, making compassion more natural and spontaneous over time.

- Expose yourself to different lives: Read books, watch documentaries, and listen to podcasts that share stories from lives vastly different from your own—refugees, farmers, single parents, prisoners, survivors. Expanding your understanding enhances your compassion.

- Remember your own moments of need: Recall a time when you felt scared, lost, hurt, or alone and someone showed you kindness. Anchoring yourself to that memory will fuel your compassion for others who are now standing where you once stood.

- Meditate on compassion: Simple daily practices like loving-kindness meditation (*May you be safe, may you be happy, may you be healthy*) can rewire the brain for greater empathy and emotional balance. Compassion, like any muscle, strengthens with exercise.

- Forgive, even when it's hard: This is one of Jesus' primary lessons. Forgiveness doesn't imply excusing harm; instead, it involves releasing yourself from the heavy burden of anger, which dulls your ability to feel compassion. Forgiving creates space in your heart once more.

- See yourself with compassion too: We cannot give what we refuse to offer ourselves. Practice treating your mistakes and pain with gentleness rather than cruelty. Self-compassion builds the foundation from which compassion for others naturally flows.

Compassion isn't just a feeling; it's a way of moving through the world. It's a muscle we can choose to strengthen every day—through attention, patience, imagination, and courageous kindness. The more we practice, the more naturally it becomes the heartbeat beneath everything we do.

How Compassion Affects the Physiology of the Human Body

Compassion isn't just an emotion; it actually changes the body on a physiological level in ways that protect and heal us. When we practice or experience compassion, several significant shifts occur within us.

It activates the "caregiving system." When we feel compassion, the brain shifts from a state of fear and threat to a caregiving mode.

Key areas of the brain light up, especially the anterior cingulate cortex (linked to emotion regulation) and the ventral vagus nerve (part of the parasympathetic nervous system—the "rest and connect" system).

This caregiving activation lowers the heart rate, regulates breathing, and fosters a sense of warmth and calmness. It effectively soothes the nervous system.

Compassion reduces cortisol levels, the body's primary stress hormone._This is important because prolonged high cortisol can damage the immune system, heart, and even the brain._By lowering stress hormones, compassion safeguards your body from the inside out.

It boosts feel-good chemicals. Here we go with the body's feel-good chemicals again. When you act compassionately, your body releases chemicals like oxytocin (the "bonding hormone"), dopamine (the "reward hormone"), and endorphins (natural painkillers).

These chemicals make you feel safer, more connected, and happier. This is why helping others often leaves you with a literal physical sensation of warmth or lightness.

Practicing compassion—especially toward yourself and others—can activate the parasympathetic nervous system, strengthen the heart, help regulate blood pressure, and improve heart rate variability (HRV).

Higher HRV indicates improved emotional resilience, better heart health, and increased life expectancy.

Studies show that compassion practices, such as loving-kindness meditation, boost the activity of protective immune cells like natural killer (NK) cells, thereby enhancing the body's immune system. When you feel more connected and less isolated, your body becomes better at fighting off illness.

The long-term practice of compassion physically reshapes the brain. MRI studies show increased thickness in areas responsible for emotional regulation, empathy, and positive emotion processing.

The more you practice compassion, the more compassionate—and physically healthier—you become.

Compassion is not just a moral good; it's a biological advantage. It soothes your nervous system, strengthens your heart, sharpens your brain, and literally helps you live longer and better. Compassion is medicine for both the giver and the receiver.

Venture outside of your comfort zone and live a life well lived.

No man ever steps in the same river twice. This profound statement by the ancient Greek philosopher Heraclitus transcends time and resonates with the ebb and flow of human existence. Within these simple words lies a deep truth about the nature of life, change, and the perpetual motion that shapes our journey.

Heraclitus invites us to reflect on the dynamic nature of our experiences. Life, like a river, is in a constant state of change and movement. Each moment is a unique intersection of circumstances, emotions, and choices. When we enter the river of time, we are immersed in a continuous flow where no two steps are identical. This timeless wisdom challenges our tendency to resist change and seek stability. Instead, it encourages us to embrace the inherent impermanence of life. The river is never the same because, as we progress, the waters around us shift, carrying us into new territories of experience and understanding.

In our personal lives, the metaphor of the river holds particular significance. Relationships evolve, careers take unexpected turns, and personal growth propels us into uncharted waters. Accepting this constant change can become a source of empowerment, fostering resilience and adaptability.

The river's symbolic depth extends to the collective human experience. Societal norms, technology, and cultural landscapes are in perpetual motion. The world we navigate today is different from yesterday, and the currents of change continue to shape our shared future. In this context, the river serves as a reminder that progress and evolution are inherent in the human story. Acknowledging the truth of Heraclitus's words offers us a lens through which to view the beauty in temporariness. Every human encounter, every physical, emotional, or spiritual challenge, and every joy is a unique blending of circumstances that will never be replicated. The river carries the richness of our diverse experiences, forming a tapestry of moments that define our individual stories and shape who we are and who we will become.

As we navigate the ever-changing currents of life, let us approach each step with mindfulness and appreciation.

Embracing the profound wisdom of this sacred truth, we uncover the freedom that comes from recognizing change as a divine journey to be celebrated. It serves as a constant reminder that, much like the flowing river, our spiritual odyssey is a dynamic and ever-unfolding adventure guided by the universe itself. So, venture forth into the vast unknown with courage in your heart. Open yourself fully and walk through every portal the cosmos presents, trusting in the path laid out before you. This embodies one essence of life's purpose. The other is to honor and follow the luminous footsteps of the enlightened souls who came before us; within their sacred texts and gentle words, you will discover the answers you seek. They are the nurturers, the bearers of peace, the intrepid seekers who embraced the wilderness, seeking adventure and the deeper truths within the great mystery of existence.

Toward the end

Life is a journey filled with ups and downs, and the struggles we face often shape us the most. But what if we could transform our challenges into a source of inspiration and service to others?

Your struggles, no matter how fearsome, are vital threads in the rich tapestry of your unique journey. Embrace them, for they have sculpted your essence and spirit. By acknowledging and embracing your experiences, you unlock the alchemy that transforms them into an epic narrative. Within every arduous battle, there are treasure troves of wisdom waiting to be discovered. Reflect on the profound lessons learned, the inner strength awakened, and the celestial insights gained along your path. These invaluable lessons are the beating heart of your story and can illuminate the way for others navigating similar quests through life's challenges.

Now, it's time to shape your story and craft your narrative. Share it in a relatable and inspiring way. Be honest about your struggles, vulnerabilities, and setbacks, but also emphasize the triumphs and growth that came from them. This authenticity will resonate with your audience and help you connect with others. One of the most powerful aspects of storytelling is its ability to bring people together. When you share your story, you create a sense of community for those who can relate. They will see that they are not alone in their struggles; this connection can be immensely comforting.

The true magic unfolds when you harness the power of your story to embark on a journey of adventure and spiritual service to others. This odyssey can manifest in countless ways—from guiding wanderers facing similar tribulations to immersing yourself in noble causes that resonate with your spirit. Your experiences transform into beacons of light, illuminating paths of hope and wisdom. By sharing your narrative and stepping into the role of a servant leader, you wield the potential to ignite profound transformations in the lives of those around you. Your journey evolves into a radiant lighthouse, demonstrating that through adversity, we can ascend to greater heights and that service can serve as a divine catalyst for goodness. Our challenges are not mere obstacles; they are sacred steppingstones toward spiritual growth and altruism. By embracing the richness of our stories, discovering the lessons woven within, and sharing them with genuine authenticity, we can create waves of positive change for those who yearn for it most. So, take the plunge today, and allow your journey to blossom into a remarkable source of inspiration and spirited service to the world.

Embrace the journey, for we are all wanderers with our vulnerabilities and moments of stumbling. Remember that our stumbles do not define us as failures; they are but steppingstones on our sacred path. Let the lessons gleaned from your trials awaken your spirit, and, with your words, become a guiding light for others. Many souls, who may be feeling weak and lost, yearn for the wisdom that lies within your adventures. Inspire them to rise and flourish in their own quests of growth and discovery.

We can all teach through our stories.

Insert 10—A Final Gift: Generations of Compassion

It was day two of Operation Smile's screening process in Guwahati, India. Hundreds of faces needed attention. John and I worked our way through the throng of people for most of the day, filming and taking note of interesting stories to follow up on later. The second day is usually half or three-quarters filled with actual patient screenings. The last bit of the day is devoted to the posting of names of those accepted for surgery. Here the names were posted on the side of the barn where the screening had taken place and, like always, this was the most emotional part of the mission. Watching parents franticly search a posted list for their child's name in a desperate crowd of others doing the same will turn your heart inside out. The experience here was no different, with exception of the large number of adults who were also looking for their own names. Among the tears of happiness and the tears of dismay there are always a couple of stories that stand out.

Here in Guwahati the heartfelt story was about a grandmother who had brought her granddaughter to the screening. Both grandmother and grandchild had been born with cleft lips. While searching the posted list of names, the grandmother saw that she had been chosen for surgery but that her granddaughter had not. With the heart of an angel, the older woman gave her surgery slip to her grandchild, saying, "I don't want you to have to go through the same difficulties in life that I have had to experience."

One of the nurses witnessed this act of compassion and dragged both generations back in front of the doctors, singing the praises of the grandmother and making sure that an extra surgery spot was created. Lessons in humanity were learned by all, and both grandmother and grandchild walked away from the mission with brand new smiles.

ABOUT THE AUTHOR

Kevin Ball is a multifaceted talent known for his contributions to the entertainment industry as a stuntman, author, and humanitarian. He gained widespread recognition for doing climatic scenes as a Creeper stunt double in the original *Jeepers Creepers* horror movie, where his iconic scenes left audiences on the edge of their seats. Kevin has lent his expertise to a plethora of blockbuster films and is now a frequent collaborator with WWE, showcasing his fearless stunts in the world of professional wrestling.

Most important to him, however, are his humanitarian efforts, which led to his founding Karma180 Productions to help non-profit organizations promote their causes and their work through video. His latest efforts focus on collaboration with communities in Rwanda.

Kevin penned the inspiring memoir *Heart of a Stuntman* (Armin Lear Press, 2022) offering readers a glimpse into the thrilling and often dangerous world of stunt work while sharing his personal journey and insights as a humanitarian. With his talent, dedication, and commitment to making a positive impact, Kevin Ball continues to leave an indelible mark on both the entertainment industry and the world at large.

www.ingramcontent.com/pod-product-compliance
Lightning Source LLC
LaVergne TN
LVHW091145080826
845145LV00008B/2261

* 9 7 8 1 9 6 8 9 1 9 3 4 4 *